HAPPINESS IS WORTH THE EFFORT

Happiness Is Worth the Effort

Elmo Ellis

HEWITT HOUSE

Old Tappan, New Jersey

Grateful acknowledgment is extended for the use of lines from *The Prophet* by Kahlil Gibran, copyright by Alfred A. Knopf, Inc. Used by permission.

Grateful acknowledgment is extended also for the quotations of Robert Frost. Used by permission of Holt, Rinehart and Winston, Inc. All rights reserved.

Grateful acknowledgment is extended for the use of lines from "Outwitted" by Edwin Markham. Used by permission of Virgil Markham.

TO MY TEACHERS

Every man is his neighbor's mentor. My instructors have been all the friends, relatives, listeners and talkers, who have made each day an exciting assignment in human relations.

For lessons in sensitivity, idealism and pride, I owe special thanks to my sister, Libby Jeanne Caplan, Dozier Cade, Glenn Perry, Ruth Kinnard, Judy Gaulden, and the late Randy Fort.

For constant companionship and counseling, I am indebted to my kids, Janet and Bryan, and my beloved wife, Ruthie.

And to you—wherever you are—special thanks for repeated reminders that happiness is worth the effort.

Contents

Introduction: What Life Is All About   11

LIVING

What Do You Want from Life?   17
Be Thankful for Troubles   20
Worry Can Be Good for You   22
Some Secrets Are for Keeping   26
You Have As Many Lives As a Cat   28
How to Unite the Family   29
Grown-Ups Shouldn't Be Too Grown-Up   31
Follow the Sunlight   34

LEARNING

What's So Great About Education?   35
Failure—A Great Teacher   40
Don't Be Too Sure   42
Ideas Have Miracle Power   45
The Lesson of the Dinosaur   46
Keep Stretching Your Mind   48

LOVE

The Meaning of Love   51
Love to Be Loved   54
Making Marriage Work   56
Loving Is Giving   59
Please Like Yourself   61
What Is Man?   63
The Healing Power of Love   65

7

RESPONSIBILITY

The Buck Stops with You 69
Freedom and Responsibility 71
The Pursuit of Responsibility 72
Be a Booster 74

IDEALISM

It's a Small World 77
No Time for Do-Nothings 79
Your Mission in Life 80

DISCIPLINE

One More Round 83
Remember to Forget 84
Winning Arguments Without Arguing 86
The Loser 87
A Challenge to Youth 88

SENSITIVITY

Sharpen Up Your Sensitivity 93
Join the Golden Rule Club 95
Try a Little Tenderness 97
The Right to Privacy 99
How Prejudiced Are You? 101
Seeing in the Dark 105

ACHIEVEMENT

You Must Climb Mountains 107
One Step at a Time 109
Flattery Will Get You Somewhere 112
You Can Overcome Handicaps 116
And Then Some 118

ETHICS

Calling All Thieves 121
The Greatest Charity 124
The Good Person 126
"His Word Was His Bond" 128
Ego and Conscience 129
Do What Is Right 130

HUMAN RELATIONS

Keep Collecting Friends   135
"The Times They Are A-Changing"   139
The Bigots Among Us   144
One Man's Junk Pile Is Another's Treasure   147

CHANGE

The Eleventh Commandment   149
Turning Points   153
Keep On Keeping On   155

AWARENESS

Are Kids Really Confusing?   157
Keep Your Cool   158
You Look Great   161
Be Proud   164
Take Your Time   166

REAL HAPPINESS

The Search for Real Happiness   169
The Most Important Day in Your Life   172
How to Have a Happy Family   173
The Simple Life   177
Learn to Laugh   179

FAITH AND THE FUTURE

How Religious Are You?   183
Prayers That Work   185
End of the World   186
Ideas for Tomorrow   188

9

Introduction:
What Life Is All About

Life has been called a game, a struggle, a combination of disappointments and pleasures. It has also been termed a picture that each of us must paint, a search for identity, and a way station between birth and immortality.

In trying to figure out what living is all about, I have become intrigued with what it is and is not. I have decided, for example, that life is a dynamic process rather than a sum of years, and it is most rewarding when we are least conscious of demanding concessions from it. Life is reaction, rather than action, reflection rather than projection. It has meaning only when interpreted in terms of human relationships, which are neither wholly perfect nor imperfect.

Ilya Ehrénburg, the Russian journalist, has recalled going around at the age of 16, repeating the words of Ibsen, "All or nothing." Later he learned that life does not offer a choice between everything and nothing. It is always somewhere in between, he found. Indeed it is. Cruelty is understandable to us because we know kindness, and madness has a meaning because it is opposed by sanity. Hate teaches us love. Ugliness makes us realize the dimensions of beauty. Bad exalts good, and immobility gives meaning to change.

Living is a balancing act in which we measure the importance of every experience by where it fits between right and wrong, sadness and happiness, failure and success. Tears teach us the worth of laughter, and all of our moments oscillate in varying degrees from sorrow to joy.

The more we learn about life, the more questions we are tempted to ask. There will always be mystery associated with tomorrow, the unknown, the unexperienced, but this ought to make our existence

11

interesting and exciting, rather than dull and tedious. We should find life fascinating but not fearful—its changing complexities not a source of disillusionment but of exciting possibilities.

D. H. Lawrence regretted that he could not live two lives: "The first in which to make one's mistakes, and the second in which to profit by them." I disagree, and suggest that we need to appreciate mistakes for the friendly allies they are—not something to be resented, but to be accepted with warm appreciation.

Suppose you couldn't make a mistake? Just imagine that everything you tried, you could do with the utmost ease. What if there were nothing to puzzle, tease or torment you? If you had no struggles, moments of indecision or desperation, then you would never experience the thrill of victory. If life were safe and foolproof, it would be unbearably dull. An error-free existence would be frightful. Only by wondering, doubting, hoping, and failing, can you know the pleasure of succeeding. It is this pairing off of opposites in the natural order of man's environment that gives meaning to human existence. We must battle the unknown, or we have no reason to exist.

Joshua Loth Liebman in *Hope For Man,* noted that "Many are the shadows that everyone carries with him. The art of living is to learn how to fill out shadows and to deal with them." Since man is capable of analyzing, interpreting and making decisions, he undergoes a continual learning experience. He is forever the student, eternally absorbing impressions and making adjustments to his environment. The world itself is a school, and everyone in it is both teacher and pupil. We cannot skip roll call, for the entire earth is our classroom, and each day is a session we must attend. If we wish, we can make our "school days" profitable and inspiring by storing up knowledge, sharpening our sensitivity and increasing our capacity to understand, to communicate, and to share the earth's blessings.

Since every generation must relearn what is lost with the passing of the preceding generation, our responsibility is a great one, made more demanding by the rapidly changing times in which we live.

In many instances, however, about the time we gain some perspective and self-assurance, so that we can begin to comprehend and cope with life, our allotted years are gone. Life must not be put off for enjoying, like a vacation, at a later date. Living is for now.

"He has spent his life best who has enjoyed it most," wrote Samuel Butler. He added, "God will take care that we not enjoy it any more than is good for us." With mortality itself as our only unconquerable

12

limitation, shouldn't we make life a joyous opening of locked doors, an awakening of minds, a joining of hearts and hands?

Every person we meet can teach us to be more aware of each human being as someone unique and priceless. Learning this can help us to become more forgiving, more generous, more kindly toward all our partners on this planet, whatever their names, wherever they live.

The famous Greek architect Constantin A. Doxiadis, has declared: "There is one way that leads to a worthy life: Man must be a good receiver, a good processor, and a good transmitter." If he doesn't pass along to others what he has assimilated, man has reached a dead end and is of no value to himself or his fellow man.

Does man need to be useful? I am convinced that it is necessary. Man is a doing creature. He has to be engaged with his fellow human beings in working on something rewarding, or he cannot be contented.

You will find in these pages ideas about being and doing. Each is a lesson of sorts, for it attempts to say something about you and your opportunities as a "student" in the "school of life."

If you are discouraged or unhappy, some of these thoughts may help you to understand yourself better, and show you how to create more positive, constructive living habits.

If you are displeased with someone, perhaps these pages will provide insight into how you can improve your relationship.

If you feel weighted down by real or imaginary handicaps, you may find some comforting suggestions about how to live with your problems and make them stepping stones to satisfying progress.

Finally, I trust that you will accept these lessons on living as they were intended: friendly reminders that the world needs you. All over this earth your "relatives,"—friends, strangers, loved ones—want to know you better and work with you more closely. They are waiting for you to prove how capable and helpful you can be, how much love and understanding you are willing to share. Show them and win yourself a heaping measure of happiness.

HAPPINESS IS WORTH THE EFFORT

Living

What Do You Want from Life?

Thousands of people commit suicide every year, many of them leaving notes declaring that life no longer has any meaning or purpose.

A double tragedy occurs every time someone takes his life. Not only does the victim cruelly and abruptly wish himself out of existence, but his talents are lost to the world because of a lie.

Life does have meaning and purpose. Every person was born for a good reason and has a role to play in the master plan of the universe. Goethe compared life to a quarry, out of which we are to mold, chisel and complete a character. Life is also a marvelous, mysterious voyage awaiting those who have the spirit and the courage to complete the trip.

Just look around at the unfinished work of the world, and you can see our reason for being. We must not take too lightly the precious awareness we have been granted, nor should we deny its potential and promise.

"Man is not the creature of circumstances," said Disraeli. "Circumstances are the creatures of man." Everyone has an obligation to change his opportunities into accomplishments.

Specifically, what you do is not so important as being actively engaged in doing something wholesome and worthwhile. How much you do is also not as vital as how honestly and conscientiously you carry out your duties. By involving yourself each day in jobs that need to be done, and then completing each one in a satisfactory manner, you will compile a record of service that will warm your heart and endear you to others.

Indeed, you can put meaning into every moment simply by deciding what you want out of life, and how much you are willing to give in return. For make no mistake about it, you must pay a price for anything you receive in this world. The depressed soul seeking oblivion pays with his life. The optimist who craves happiness, earns it with service to his fellow man.

There are individuals who instinctively understand what it means to pursue a purposeful career. When Dr. Albert Schweitzer chose to spend his years helping the helpless in Africa, he was answering a summons to service that was perfectly clear in his mind. He never regretted the decision because he remained at his medical mission despite repeated entreaties to lure him elsewhere.

There's a grandmother in Georgia who volunteered at the age of seventy for the Peace Corps and spent two years working with lepers in India. She found every hardship an enriching experience, and the satisfaction she derived from nursing the sick and assisting the needy made her feel younger and more joyful than she had in years.

Life takes on new dimensions when we seek out the needy and then pitch in to be of help to them. This is one way to put new pep into anyone's life in a hurry!

Many youngsters complain that they can find no place for themselves in the world because they are repelled by the hypocrisy, cruelty, discrimination, and indifference they encounter. But is anyone more guilty of these faults than the person who refuses to get involved, claiming that the rules of life and the ways people behave aren't to his liking? Although ours is an imperfect society run by imperfect people, we can improve things for ourselves and others simply by turning our dissatisfaction into constructive action.

18

If you have come to a crossroads in your own life and you feel dissatisfied and confused about your future, why not sit down and try to decide precisely what you want to do? What would it take to make you feel happier and more productive? Are you active enough in church, in civic groups, in charitable organizations? Is your job bringing you a sense of importance and fulfillment? Are you spending enough time with your family?

Try jotting on a sheet of paper some of the goals you want to reach. Make a timetable, indicating what you would like to accomplish this year, and for the next five or ten years. Try not to be too self-centered in your ambitions, because if you expect to succeed at anything you must do it with the help and cooperation of others.

As you write down your objectives, be specific and include both major and minor ones, the serious and the not-so-serious. Keep in mind that you may find more happiness by becoming a reader for the blind, a good dancer or bridge player than by accumulating a fortune in stocks and bonds.

Above all, never allow yourself to think that your life is too small and simple to matter. Setting goals in life is not for a chosen few. This is a game that everyone can and should play.

Even if you are a housewife or a farmer in the remotest village, you can still lead a life rich in service and brimming with happiness. I know a young author, so crippled from arthritis, that he must write slowly, painfully, a few words at a time. Nevertheless, he cheerfully turns out one successful article after another. Just by carrying on as he does, this writer is an inspiration to everyone he meets.

Doubtlessly, you also possess abilities that can impress and benefit others. Everyone is a walking storehouse of creativity, with the capacity to make the world a better place for his having lived in it. You need only believe in yourself and apply your talents to prove it.

Thomas Wolfe emphasized the dividends we collect when we do our best.

"If a man has a talent and cannot use it, he has failed," wrote Wolfe. "If he has a talent and uses only half of it, he has partly failed. If he has a talent and learns somehow to use the whole of it, he has gloriously succeeded, and won a satisfaction and a triumph few men ever know."

What talents are you failing to use? How much satisfaction are you losing? What triumphs are you sacrificing? Remember, every person must choose daily whether to hide his talents fearfully and selfishly, or use them unselfishly and optimistically.

If you choose to chart a course of useful and constructive activity, you will find that you can succeed at new jobs. You can develop friendships, contribute to community projects, and prove yourself capable and helpful in ways that you may have never dreamed possible.

It all starts with two simple questions: What do you want from life? What are you willing to give?

Be Thankful for Troubles

Everybody complains about troubles; but what if suddenly you found yourself transported to a magical Shangri-La where cares and confusion didn't exist, what would you do? I can tell you that in short order you'd get nervous and so unhappy that you'd invent your first bit of trouble. You would begin to worry because there was nothing to worry about!

When you think objectively about adversity, you realize that a certain amount of it is inevitable and perhaps even beneficial. It has been observed, "Nobody ever grew despondent looking for trouble." Certainly problems can keep us so occupied that they fill an important place in our lives.

Novelist Ellen Glasgow noted that some women like to sit down to trouble as if it were knitting. Who doesn't know at least one solemn and sad-eyed sufferer who always wants to tell about his terrible problems? I have always thought that such individuals needed troubles the way an addict requires dope. Instead of trying to forget his cares, the chronic complainer prides himself on remembering every painful moment of agony and indecision he has ever experienced.

We have all heard stories about hermits living far away in the hills, safe from annoyances and free of worries—but these are strictly fairy tales. Even on the most remote mountaintop a person must relate to something: to his fellow man, to a faithful dog or donkey, to his memories, or to God. The moment anyone's mind latches onto a natural or supernatural question, he becomes alert, curious and involved. From this awareness grows a feeling of anxiety, and the ability to dwell on and solve problems.

Horace, the Roman poet, declared, "Adversity has the effect of eliciting talents which in prosperous circumstances would have lain dormant." Troubles have a way of alerting and arming us for battle. Mishaps can sharpen the mind, toughen the will and strengthen determination. Man was not meant to be a puppet, incapable of deciding his own fate. He has developed as a creature fully capable of cooking up difficulties for himself and figuring how to get out of them. This requires not only reasoning ability, but the capacity to be concerned—so be thankful for your worries. They are the fair price you must pay for the right fully to play the game of life.

Edith Sitwell once jested, "Hot water is my native element; I was in it as a baby, and I have never seemed to get out of it ever since." This pretty well describes most of us. We skip from one problem to another because that's part of living from one day to the next. But if you think of impediments as opportunities, and difficulties as doors to be opened, you realize that every pesky situation can have a meaning and value far beyond its solution. Troubles can be the tools that we use to fashion a better future for ourselves and everyone around us.

Worry Can Be Good for You

Do you worry a great deal?

If so, thank the Lord for giving you the ability and awareness to be concerned. Worry is a sign of sanity and maturity.

People don't go to the psychiatrist because they worry too much. They go because they don't know how to worry and have become overwhelmed by confusion and impotence.

I get impatient with members of the tranquilizer crowd who insist that worry is a demon and must be avoided at all costs. That makes about as much sense as having someone recommend that you quit breathing because in consuming oxygen you are burning up your lungs.

What causes you to worry? Think about a typical day and sort out in your mind the things that upset you. Everyone worries at times about loving and being loved. We all worry if we feel misunderstood or unappreciated. It's pretty universal to worry about health, safety and security. Though we shouldn't dwell on matters we cannot control, most of us do worry considerably about past mistakes, present-day obstacles and future possibilities.

Although some of my friends seem to take pride in being champion worriers, I'm not sure that this is an ability at all. In a sense, worrying is simply a natural reaction of all thinking creatures to unanswered questions and unopened doors which they are reluctant to enter.

Our poodle worries terribly if he sees my wife preparing to give him a bath or a clip. Cats worry when strange dogs come near. I cite these examples to emphasize that being able to worry is no proof of intellectual prowess, but it is most certainly a normal part of living. Furthermore, if you elect to get aroused about matters beyond the realm of your own personal interests, then worrying can even take on distinctive and noble qualities.

Obviously, for anyone who wants to try his hand at positive worrying, there's plenty to contemplate and to tantalize creative energies. Never have we faced so many riddles that needed solving. Never has mankind had so many massive forces working to undermine his sanity and safety.

Good solid worry and intelligent response may be the strongest weapons we can marshall to master our toughest problems. And take heart, for in getting yourself worked up about the miscellaneous miseries of your fellow man, you may just discover a recipe for better health and a more composed mind.

The only thing wrong with worrying is what people let it do to them. If you have become a chronic worrier and feel helpless because of it, then you're misusing a valuable asset and allowing it to abuse you. It's sad to know that so many hospital patients are worry casualties, immobilized by agitation and anxiety, when they should be spurred by worry to get a lot done and feel great at the same time.

Any time you begin to feel trapped by problems you cannot master, don't throw up your hands in despair. Worry is not something to resist frantically or to suffer with a heavy heart. Instead, try to think about worry the way a race horse owner accepts a weight handicap. If you are capable of carrying a bit more of the load, do it and profit from the experience.

Worrying need never be a villainous, self-defeating process. It can actually be both stimulating and therapeutic. Most of the energetic, well-adjusted people I know are excellent worriers. There is, however, a special way to do your worrying. It involves not only adopting a positive attitude but using the right techniques to make worries work for you instead of against you.

Consider first that daily disturbances almost always appear most awesome when they first zoom into view. So it's a good idea to analyze any chafing situation that arises to see if your uneasiness is even justified.

I remember an old checker player in my home town who was always singing the praises of worry. "Don't tell me worrying doesn't do any good," he would argue. "I know better. The things I worry about don't happen." That makes sense, doesn't it?

We should take comfort from realizing that most of the problems we dread having to contend with never materialize, and a great many that do arise are little more than nuisances waiting to be swatted like so many flies.

"The cares of today are seldom those of tomorrow," suggested

Cowper. "And when we lie down at night we may safely say to most of our troubles, 'Ye have done your worst, and we shall see you no more.' "

What should you do though when unsettled business does pile up on you? How can you keep burdens and vexations under control? A mere change of routine often works wonders. Anxiety seems to melt away from anyone who is engrossed with new ideas, sorting out and relishing a raft of fresh experiences.

Recreation is also an answer to overburdening tension. However, whether you try to relax on a golf course, play tennis, or lose yourself in an engrossing hobby, keep in mind that competitive sports may induce anger and frustration if you are unable to make the scores you desire. Rather than get yourself worked up needlessly, it may be better to occupy your spare time with a non-competitive activity such as painting, gardening, boating or bird watching.

It's important to understand, of course, that staying busy doesn't necessarily mean that you have licked the worry phobia. Some of the most active persons I know are also among the most frantic. They constantly seem to be running without reaching the sanctuary they seek. Anyone who wants to flee from his uneasiness must treat the problem as a self-centered illness and not try to escape from what is really inside himself and is a part of him.

The best way to cure the disease of obsessive worry, says psychoanalyst Erich Fromm, is to find an adequate center around which you can organize yourself. Jumping from one activity to another won't do it. Basic calmness and poise must be developed internally as replacements for fear and uncertainty.

As you develop self-confidence and learn to deal with the unpleasant as well as the pleasant obligations of each day, you will find that worries do have a place in your life, but not a throne from which to rule.

Worries get out of hand only when we allow them to take over and dictate to us. This happens most often to the person who is poorly organized. Decide clearly what you intend to get done each day. Try your hand at putting priority on the jobs that are most important and finishing them first. You may be surprised to find that organization and planning can do much to lighten burdens, level out exasperations, and enable you to get a great deal done with a minimum of concern.

24

Now what about the worry that eludes your best corrective action? We all know that worries develop in many forms and for many reasons; and some are so pesky they cannot be conquered, tamed or ignored. What then should you do? I would recommend that you endeavor to meet whatever is plaguing you face-to-face. Bring the unresolved question out in the open so you can see it clearly, turn it around, and examine it from all sides, and face a showdown.

"The block of granite which was an obstacle in the pathway of the weak," Carlyle declared, "becomes a stepping stone in the pathway of the strong." You literally can defeat most of the worries in your life by taking them apart, piece by piece, and turning them into opportunities.

Next time you get stuck on the horns of a dilemma that you can't comprehend or successfully wrestle into submission, talk the situation over with a trusted friend or loved one. An additional viewpoint is oftentimes just what is needed to bring a big worry into focus so you can take aim on it.

Still another way to cope with worry is to brush up on the subject that's plaguing you. When you study a problem and thoroughly understand it, you cease to be afraid of it. You can gain insight by reading books on topics that trouble you. In the process, you may find more than the answer you need. What has haunted you as a dark, despairing difficulty may turn into a fascinating and attractive new field of investigation and opportunity.

One final suggestion for making your life more enjoyable and less hectic—learn how to enjoy worry. That's right, you can do this, even though at first it might appear impossible. Worrying done in a positive and responsible manner can stir the blood, jog the mind and give you a renewed awareness of your importance.

Think how dull the world would be if there were nothing worth fretting about. I suspect that the colossal boredom of having no worries would quickly send the most docile soul out in search of a few cares just to make life interesting!

Some Secrets Are for Keeping

Do you find it difficult to keep a secret?

Are you the type of husband or wife who feels that you must share everything you know with your partner? If so, take a bow for your intentions, but don't kid yourself that it's happening. No one is capable of sharing everything he knows with another, regardless of the closeness of their relationship; besides, it is impossible to find anyone who would dare tell everything he knew, even to the person he loved and trusted most dearly.

In other words, we all have some secrets; and even the woman who keeps appointments faithfully with her psychiatrist reserves a few matters to be left unsaid.

If you think this is bad, that we should be completely honest and aboveboard with one another, ask yourself what would happen if we really did open the floodgates and let all the secrets out? Life would be a madhouse; every marriage in America would probably dissolve overnight and lifelong friendships would be wrecked on the rocks of bitter truth.

Secrets have for centuries been misunderstood and maligned. "Never suffer a thought to be harbored in your mind which you would not avow openly." Thomas Jefferson uttered that noble and downright impractical suggestion, but even he never made such frank and total revelations because it wasn't always practical or desirable. For various sound and logical reasons, every human being stores away a certain number of secrets, some of which he probably carries with him to the grave.

Hamlet had the right idea. "Give thy thoughts no tongue;" especially thoughts better left unsaid. At least one modern expert has come to the defense of the much-abused secret, even endorsing it as a means of creating happier marriages. English psychologist, Dr. John Cohen, says that nothing else keeps a marriage so alive and interesting as a few well-kept secrets.

"In the newly-wed days there is a great temptation to yield everything in total abandon, leaving nothing in reserve," he explains. "This can be fraught with danger, because only those persons who are capable of constantly creating something fresh can afford to give themselves entirely.

"Most human beings have limited mental and emotional resources. If you constantly reveal your innermost thoughts and feelings, there may come a time when one or the other will be emptied. Many a marriage has been wrecked because there was no room for novelty."

Engaged and married couples sometimes play a tricky game of trying to wring secrets out of one another. Often the devious and persistent questions refer to former suitors and girl friends. "Were you in love?" "How much?" "What did you do together?" If carried too far, this kind of interrogation may bring out secrets that both parties will regret.

Virtually everyone harbors in his memory a former romance, a shameful episode, a regrettable mistake, a dark moment of doubt. All of these are part of the experiences of everyday living, and some are too tender or painful to be related to anyone. Telling might make things rather lively around the house, but declining to tell can add a fascinating bit of mystery; and that is often safer and more desirable.

Generally, the kind of secret to protect is the one that would hurt someone if exposed. Sometimes we hear a juicy bit of gossip about a person; and whether it is true or not, passing it along could only be harmful. Perhaps you've observed a questionable act, or discovered some information that is not flattering. Unless you have a legal or moral obligation to reveal it, forget it.

Some people reveal useless, or even harmful, secrets about themselves when it isn't necessary. This occurs frequently with the individual who is conscience-stricken, or so desirous of attention that he is willing to demean himself to be noticed.

Once you tell a secret that was better left untold, you invariably experience feelings of remorse as it flies away to begin its malicious mischief. As long as you hold tightly to a secret, it is your prisoner and you are its master. But if you let it go, then the secret assumes command and you are its prisoner.

So keep at least a few choice bits of intelligence locked up, even from the ones nearest and dearest to you. And don't worry if this means that there is a part of you that goes unshared with the one you love most. No person gives all of himself to another. The closest relationship is still a limited partnership. The number of secrets shared or withheld is not what makes or breaks a human relationship. What really matters is that you make no secret of your love and respect for one another, for that is the cement that binds two hearts together.

You Have as Many Lives as a Cat

How many lives do you have? Is it one; or, like the proverbial cat, are you really blessed with nine lives that you have never counted?

Everyone has a childhood. This is different from any other life you have. It is a unique set of experiences, and from it you learn a whole set of special lessons that prepare you for an entirely different existence to follow. So much for life *number one*.

After they are grown, most men have a business or professional life; and so do many career women. Wives and mothers who stay at home usually have a very busy life keeping house and caring for children. In either case, this provides a long and often a very full and productive career, accounting for life *number two*.

We all have a home life that is unique in its meaning for us. We can embrace not only family members in the circle of our affection, but as many friends as we wish. And moments shared can provide a lifetime of pride and joy. That's life *number three*.

Everyone has some kind of religious life. In many of the rebellious it is hidden or denied, but faith is still there and will of a certainty express itself in allegiance to a power or a cause greater than the individual. Who among us could deny that his spiritual life is a unique part of his existence as a human being? That makes life *number four*.

There is also available to us a civic and social life. For many it may express itself principally in attending luncheon clubs and PTA meetings. For others, it may be more serious pursuits, such as entering politics or doing welfare work. This comprises life *number five*.

The recreational life that we lead is in many ways completely apart from the remainder of our existence. Depending on each person's interests, we spend countless hours playing. Preferences range from hunting, golfing and fishing to gardening, reading, watching TV or listening to radio. For many the leisure life is the principal one pursued. Count this as life *number six*.

Then there is the life of rest. For most persons it requires approximately a third of every day, devoted to sleep and relaxation. This is your *seventh life*.

Apart from the dreaming that we do when asleep, there is another dream life of sorts that we all know. It is the Walter Mitty in us encouraging frequent excursions into a never-never-land where we can give full play to our imagination. This is life *number eight*.

Finally, there's a complete life that everyone experiences in the world of memory. As each day passes by, it leaves a residue of recollections. These we store for reference purposes and for the sheer enjoyment of remembering and comparing yesterday with today. That's life *number nine*.

So there they are: nine lives available for the taking. Nine lives that we can make colorful, vital and worthy of prideful recognition. Nine lives that should be measured not by their length, but by how full and satisfying we make them, living courageously and compassionately, giving the best we have to offer to our fellow men, and getting in return a world of happiness.

How to Unite the Family

A graduate student doing research on juvenile delinquency at the University of Wisconsin reported considerable difficulty in collecting data. His project was to telephone a dozen homes at night around nine o'clock and ask parents if they knew where their children were at this hour.

"My first five calls," he lamented, "were answered by children who had no idea where their parents were."

Perhaps this is an exaggerated case, but then again, maybe not.

Parents and their children are constantly being separated from one another, not just physically, but in other ways as well. Many youngsters don't even try nowadays to talk to their fathers because they say the old man is a square, or he's unreasonable, or he's just not interested. Mom and the kids often have similar difficulties in conversing with one another.

How can this happen, you may wonder, when parents and children are living together under the same roof? Why this gulf of alienation? If the problem is greater today than in past years, why is it?

One big answer must simply be that grown-ups forget too easily what it means to be young. Adults think they remember, but all they may recall are a few colorful childhood incidents. What is most critical—and what they have forgotten—are juvenile feelings and fears, the adolescent's uncertainties and inhibitions, his longing for recognition and self-esteem, and his strong inclination to pledge allegiance to his idols and his ideals, regardless of the consequences.

The youngster on the other hand has never been able (and perhaps never will be able) to understand what grown-up responsibilities are until he grows into them. Meanwhile, crises may occur when the son or daughter who feels he cannot communicate with his elders lets it be known through a variety of rebellious acts that serve only to further divide the family.

Healthful responsibilities can be assigned, however, to anyone of any age. If every family member had definite duties, and was held accountable for them, knowing that the good performance would be rewarded and applauded, family living might well begin to assume some of its former importance and lustre.

Margaret Meade has declared that society has found no permanent substitute for the family as a way of shaping whole human beings. We might ask though, do enough parents still believe this? Do they believe it enough and want it enough to make the home and the family a center of more shared fun, with more give-and-take, more discussions and decisions? Homes can be (and should be) meeting places of love and faith, where family members do much more listening to one another—and communicating with one another—in quiet moments of intimacy and sympathetic concern.

Grown-Ups Shouldn't Be Too Grown-Up

Once when he was Prime Minister of India, Pandit Nehru confessed that his solemn, aristocratic appearance was somewhat misleading. "I have always found my troubles hardest to handle when I let the grown-up in me get the better of me." He went on to explain that he was most capable of dealing with the monumental duties of leading a nation of 400 million when he retained a youthful outlook and a childlike sense of humor. Never take yourself too seriously, he warned.

It may seem strange to think that this statesman and international leader could have uttered such words, but Nehru often looked much gloomier than he felt. While suffering through a boring speech one time at an Indian Congress Party Convention, the celebrated leader picked up a huge pillow and threw it at one of the nodding delegates, hitting him squarely in the face, much to the merriment of the crowd.

As a natural leader, he knew the importance of keeping his followers interested; and he would surprise them into alertness at times with a bit of juvenile horseplay. He knew that grown-ups shouldn't feel or act grown-up every moment of their lives.

General Dwight Eisenhower was another famous personality who knew how to act younger than his years and make it pay off. During World War II, he spoke one day at an outdoor assembly of GI's. As he left the platform from which he had delivered his remarks, Eisenhower slipped and fell in the mud. The surprised soldiers caught their breath and then roared with laughter. Later in recounting the episode, Eisenhower explained how he had turned the accident into an advantage by laughing with the troops at his plight: "You know, of all the things I said and did to raise the morale of those boys, it was that fall on the seat of my pants which did them the most good."

As the nation's Chief Executive, Eisenhower was working one day at his White House desk when his grandson, David, came in and asked an executive assistant, "Is he working?"

The President looked up and smiled, "David," he said, "I only do this for fun."

It was literally true, for the world-renowned general did try to make his working hours a source of fun and pleasure; and he was rarely too busy to hear a good joke or tell one. He was especially fond of recalling anecdotes about his boyhood, revealing in each account his ever-youthful spirit.

When he was President of the United States, Harry Truman also consistently proved that he was a young-at-heart jokester, prankster and wit. Just before he left for the historic Potsdam Conference, he wrote to his mother: "I am getting ready to see Stalin and Churchill and it is a chore. I have to take my tuxedo, tails, preacher coat, high hat, low hat and hard hat."

Truman kidded newsmen constantly, and occasionally he would compose a whimsical memorandum that exhibited just how youthfully devilish he could be. Just before Christmas, 1947, he wrote: "I have appointed a Secretary of Semantics—a most important post. He is to furnish me forty-to-fifty dollar words, tell me how to say yes and no in the same sentence without a contradiction. He is to tell me the combination of words that will put me against inflation in San Francisco and for it in New York. He is to show me how to keep silent—and say everything. You can very well see how he can save me an immense amount of worry."

A study of the American presidents and their writings reveals that all had a sense of humor, some sharp and some gentle. John Adams loved to tell off-color jokes. Scholarly Woodrow Wilson enjoyed composing humorous limericks.

Calvin Coolidge was once asked, "Mr. President, do the people where you come from say 'A hen lays' or 'A hen lies'?"

Coolidge's reply was simply: "The people where I come from, sir, lift her up to see."

Many others among the world's most serious-minded leaders have been gifted with boyish charm and a penchant for practical jokes. John F. Kennedy was notorious for teasing his friends and disparaging himself.

Mark Twain typified the man of great intellect who always managed never to become too grown-up. He wrote some of the most devastating satire in American literature, but he also authored those classic characters of perpetual youth, Tom Sawyer and Huckleberry Finn.

Will Rogers was another humorist who never quit smiling and remained eternally young in the minds of his millions of admirers.

Anyone who can deal with serious matters without taking himself too seriously is capable of exerting great influence. It is an art to know when to smile or laugh and break the tension of a crucial meeting. The most gifted leader is the one who is not impressed with his power or importance, but rather fancies himself a catalyst, capable of bringing together divergent groups and interests.

How seriously do you take yourself? Are you inclined to worry too much about your responsibilities? Do you fret over trivial details? And do you find yourself fighting tension with tension, feeling old and tired and worn-out from battling alone against ever-increasing pressures? If the answers are yes, it's quite likely that you are playing life not as an intriguing and adventurous game, but as a succession of crises in which there is no time for levity or nonsense.

Why not loosen up and mix a little pleasure with the pain? Jimmy Durante appears to millions as a man ripe in years and still as lovable and innocent as a child. It is no pretense. The humble entertainer acts the way he feels. He is young at heart. He once told a reporter: "I don't want anything else. I've got my family, my health. I thank God every morning for both. I like to make people laugh. Dey like me. What could I want? I don't want all da money in da world."

We may be young only once, but you can stay young in your attitude, your opinions, and your outlook on life. You can think young. You can feel young. And you can be youthfully enthusiastic about everything you do.

Follow the Sunlight

Did you ever watch a dog or cat follow a patch of sunlight on a winter's day, as the warm rays moved across the living room floor in a narrow beam? No matter how thin the patch of light, your pet manages, if he is so inclined, to keep in the sunshine and to absorb its warmth.

I once heard a minister, Dr. Clarence Showalter, telling of such an incident that he had observed in a backwoods cabin in Wisconsin. The trees were so dense that only a thin streak of sunlight was able to penetrate. But his dog, Blackie, was faithfully keeping his coat warm by basking in the sunlight and moving with it.

As Dr. Showalter put it, "Few of us have lives that are all sunshine. But none of us has a life without its patch of sunlight." It's up to us though to keep moving into the sunlit spots. The sunshine will not wait for you. You must move with it, otherwise you will soon be enveloped by shadows and eventually by the darkness of night itself.

One of the saddest commentaries on our present way of life is to know that countless patients fill rows of beds in hospitals all over this country because they suffer from nervous troubles and emotional disorders. A principal cause of all this illness is that many people lose sight of the sunshine in their lives and become weighted down to the breaking point by accumulated problems, fears and frustrations.

If we could look the disturbed among us in the eye, we might try to convince them that the past is gone and cannot be relived, and the future is yet to be conquered and should not be dreaded but anticipated.

This leaves only the present. Today and this moment are ours to fill with as much joy and hope, sunshine and optimism, as we are able to seek out and enjoy.

If we will only keep moving with the sunlight, we can add a great deal of brightness to our lives.

Learning

What's So Great About Education?

Dear Student:

You ask me why you have to go to school, and you wonder what's so great about education?

I can recall raising the same questions when I was a boy, especially on cold, winter mornings when the bed was warm; and it would have been much nicer to sleep than to trudge to school for a long day of writing papers, listening to lectures and taking tests.

What is this education business all about? Why should it be emphasized so much when it isn't half as much fun as playing in a tree house, or going fishing, or loafing around with your pals?

In the first place, I don't think you ought to be required to spend six or eight hours going to classes just to be bored and unhappy. I happen to believe that education can be and ought to be a good thing, as good and as much fun as a football game or a sock hop or watching television. As a matter of fact, all of these activities are part of learning, just as much as when you are in a classroom.

So maybe school isn't fun simply because a lot of people don't really know what getting an education is all about; (and I include among the confused, millions of mamas, daddies and teachers, as well as students).

One thing is for sure: if anyone says that you have to go to school just because you're *supposed* to—or because *all* kids go to school—that's *not* a good reason.

Or, if you have a teacher who tells you that you *have* to go to school to memorize the contents of some books and learn how to read and write and work problems, these aren't good enough reasons either. In fact, it isn't even necessary to go to school to learn how to make a living. You could probably grow up and manage to make *some* kind of living even if you never went to school another day.

And what if you are told that you have to go to school so that you can prepare yourself to be rich and prominent? I don't think much of that reason. It's not that I have anything against your becoming wealthy and famous someday, but that's not the mission of the school. Plenty of affluent and powerful people in this world are neither successful nor happy.

There's one other faulty reason sometimes given for going to school. We hear people say that school is a place where you learn that life is no bed of roses. They seem to think that studies should be dull and tough and boring if they are to do you any good.

The argument seems to be the one I used to hear as a kid about taking medicine. The more unpleasant it tasted, the better it was supposed to be for you. Now, when you think about it, that's silly, isn't it?

You shouldn't have to take education the way you take castor oil. Education should be fun. It *can* taste good. In fact, if you are really being educated, it *is* fun.

Let me tell you why I say this. I think that getting educated means learning how to deal with changes and chances. In other words, the more we learn, the better able we are to grapple with the problems and challenges and opportunities that confront us every day of our lives.

Education helps you to reason out things, to think more clearly, to make better decisions every time you have to decide what to do.

You might define education as "learning how to make sense out

36

of life." And the educational process goes on every moment that you are awake. It's incorrect to think that the only time you are being educated is when you are in school. Every person you meet, every experience you have, teaches you something, wherever you are and whatever you may be doing.

Of course, much of what you are taught is faulty. It is often incorrect information. You could learn a great deal every day just by bumming around, but much of what you absorbed would be of questionable value. It could even be dangerous and deadly.

Only an exceptional person like Abraham Lincoln, Eric Hoffer or President Harry S Truman could be expected to read and study and learn a great deal by his own efforts with a minimum of teacher-help or attendance at school.

You are fortunate. You have a fine school building, comfortable classrooms, many capable teachers, a well-stocked library, and an opportunity to do a great deal of your learning in comfortable surroundings.

I firmly believe that going to school under these conditions ought to be and can be a pleasurable adventure. Some of it should be work. Some of it should be play. And all of it should be satisfying and rewarding.

If you were to ask a member of your school's football team or basketball team how hard he had to practice, I'm sure he would tell you: "Pretty hard. But I like it."

Much of your schooling can be that way. Getting an education may be *hard* at times, but you can still *like* it; if you and your teacher make learning a fascinating kind of game and providing you both participate in the learning process. I say this because I believe that students must teach teachers, just as teachers are expected to teach students. A youngster learns very little if he merely listens to his teacher, takes notes, and then repeats at test time what the teacher has told him to remember. Consider, though, how much more you can learn if you discuss with your teacher why you are learning a particular subject and how it will be helpful to you.

This is what bugs you at times, I know. You find yourself trying to figure out what earthly use you will ever make of some of the subject matter you are required to study.

Somebody once asked Johnny Carson, the television star, what courses had been most helpful to him in his profession; and he answered: "All of them. Everything I've ever learned," he said, "I have later found useful in some way."

In similar fashion, a great scientist surprised me one day by naming the most valuable subject he had ever studied. I thought he would say mathematics or physics, or geometry. But instead, he named English. "All of the other subjects were extremely important," he said, "but English enabled me to explain my ideas so that others could understand them."

The point is simply that every bit of your schooling has a purpose. All of it *can* be useful.

Your education should deal with why you think as you do as much as what you think, and how you feel as much as how you reason.

If I had my way, all of your grades could be thrown away, providing you were learning and experiencing what you can best utilize. I don't think it's nearly as important to get a report of what you know, as it is to measure what you are in the process of becoming.

The day is long gone when a dividing line could be drawn between education for acquiring skills and education for living. The two are one and the same, just as the science of teaching and the art of learning must become one.

President Nixon has said, "When I look at American education, I do not see schools, but young Americans who deserve the chance to make a life for themselves and ensure the progress of their country."

Right now, I cannot predict the many ways you will be using what you are learning ten years from now. I'm quite sure that much of what you are studying today will be valuable, but one of the biggest problems of the educator is to estimate what you need to know and how much you can and should absorb.

This brings to mind the case of the teacher who kept giving his classes the same questions each year on the final examinations. Even though the word got around among the students, they still had trouble making good grades.

One day a student said to the teacher, "How come if we all know the questions you are going to ask, we can't all make A's?"

The teacher replied, "It's simple. The questions remain the same, but every year the answers change."

In our fast moving world, that is often the case. The questions stay the same but the answers keep changing. Regardless of whether you are in school or out of school, you will find yourself constantly having to face and solve new and perplexing problems. You will be expected to come up with new answers to such age-old questions as these:

1. How do we feed and clothe and house all of the people in the world?

2. How do we keep nations from destroying one another in deadly wars?

3. How do we clean up our rivers and lakes?

4. How do we protect the air that we breathe?

5. How do we combat the diseases that claim so many victims?

6. How do we teach one person to be fair and considerate of another person so that our cities will not become jungles of crime and corruption?

7. How do we manage to live sanely in a world that is so full of insanity?

You'll notice that I've only named a few of the biggest questions. All of the smaller questions that we must deal with at home, in school and elsewhere are related to these.

So this is what education is all about! It's learning to know more about this world, and its people, and the problems we all must share together. Education means learning how to constantly look for new and better answers, never assuming that we already know enough or that we already have the best answer.

Aristotle said many centuries ago, "It is by education I learn to do by choice what other men do by the constraint of fear."

Schools were created not to frighten you, or to bore you, or to confuse you, but to help prepare you to make choices, to give you knowledge and self-confidence and better judgment; and thus you will be able to live a life that is useful to your country, helpful to your family, friends and neighbors, and satisfying to yourself.

I urge you to keep asking your parents and teachers, "Why am I learning this? How can I use it? What does it mean?" Make each classroom session a give-and-take time for relating what is discussed to what is going on around you. If it's blowing in the wind, see if you can find out what it's saying.

I believe it was Socrates who said that you cannot teach a person anything. You can only help him find out for himself.

In finding out what you want to know, you might find these words of educator Tryon Edwards helpful: "The great end of education is to discipline, rather than to furnish the mind; to train it to the use of its own powers, rather than fill it with the accumulation of others."

Good luck, and remember that education is a continuing process of unlearning the useless as well as learning the useful. I urge you to do both every day.

Sincerely,

OVER THIRTY

Failure – A Great Teacher

Failure is a bad word and that's regrettable. It needs a better reputation because a man's best teacher can often be a good, solid failure. Certainly anyone who has failed after an honest, sincere effort may have lost an objective but gained something immeasurably greater in value—understanding of his shortcomings and how to correct them in order to achieve future victories.

Of course, it is generally a painful experience to fail, especially when others know about it. The Chinese call this losing face. There are stories of Orientals becoming so embarrassed over failures that they felt obliged to commit suicide.

Although we in the western world don't have a term to describe what it means to fail (and have your friends find out), we understand well enough what a devastating experience this can be. For a youngster, losing a school ball game or making an unsatisfactory grade on a test can reduce him to tears. For adults, failure in business, in marriage, in combat, can be soul-shattering experiences.

40

Still, it is a shame that we cannot learn to understand what failure really means so that we can accept it with much more calmness and peace of mind. Failure is simply the natural counterpart to success, and it is something that we are destined to experience many times.

Failures are not all negative and certainly it is not evil or sinful to fail. Losing doesn't necessarily prove weakness or lack of preparation. It merely means that at some point you have been checkmated and not allowed to achieve what you expected. Keats called failure, "The highway to success, inasmuch as every discovery of what is false leads us to seek earnestly after what is true, and every fresh experience points out some form of error which we shall afterward carefully avoid."

If we will only discipline ourselves to think positively about mistakes, we can learn a great deal from every vain effort. William Whewell, the English philosopher, described the process in this manner: "Every detection of what is false directs us toward what is true; every trial exhausts some tempting form of error."

Proof that failure can be a splendid teacher is indicated by the effect it leaves on the mind. The sting of disappointment, when we founder at a task we feel deeply about, impresses us more profoundly than does the joy of victory.

Virtually every celebrated author has fizzled many times. Ernest Hemingway collected rejection slips by the dozens before his stories began to sell. Often in trying to get a paragraph to read as he felt it should, Hemingway would write it over and over again, each revision a dud in his estimation, until finally the lines read as he wished them to.

Abraham Lincoln failed in almost every job he undertook until the successful race that carried him to Washington and martyrdom. Albert Einstein chalked up many more scientific failures than he did successes. Dr. Jonas Salk experimented endlessly, failing time after time, before discovering the ultimate answer to the menace of polio. In fact, scientific research and development are based not on being *right,* but on being *wrong;* for by finding what is incorrect, the experimenter eventually learns what is correct.

Life itself is a succession of failures and triumphs. You can be sure when you get out of bed each morning that the day will bring you some satisfying moments of achievement, balanced off by a certain number of setbacks. Fortunately, most of the rebuffs you must endure will prove to be minor. They may cause mosquito-like annoyance but can be quickly disposed of and forgotten. Even a major fiasco, if judged properly, can show you what went wrong and point the way to adjustments that will transform your next try into a happy ending.

The only kind of failure that is inexcusable is the loss that occurs by default when someone declines to try or hesitates to give his best effort at winning. That is the one misfortune in life that has no happy ending, because it represents the tragedy of a person without ambition or sense of responsibility.

The individual who cannot control his weaknesses and inhibitions may very well give up before he begins. His lack of confidence is the assurance of his defeat. On the other hand, if you can teach yourself to be unafraid of failing—and actually welcome a set-back as a lesson in experience—you will be on your way to a more enjoyable future, filled with fascinating failures and exciting successes.

Don't Be Too Sure

Have you ever thought how much you take for granted each day?

Most of us assume that we will wake up feeling fit, that the world will still be intact, and all familiar landmarks will be in their proper places.

We expect light to flood the room when we flip a switch. There is no doubt in our mind that water will flow when the faucet is turned on or that the radio will bring forth music at our command.

Your car is supposed to start when you turn a key, and it usually does without fail. Driving to work or going shopping, you feel quite confident that you will get through the traffic jams without an accident and make it to your destination on time.

Unless frightened by pain or illness, you have little doubt that your heart will keep beating and that your mind will manage to make sense of all that you experience.

Living is a constant process of believing that what we expect to happen will happen. In time we may even become over-confident and think that virtually everything and everyone can be expected to follow a predictable course.

It is true that the world does look about the same from one day to the next, but it is one day older, one day different. From the time we go to bed at night until we get up in the morning, many things have drastically changed. If you have ever been isolated for a few weeks from newspapers, radio and television, you know what a shock it can be to learn how much has taken place. There have been accidents, upheavals of nature, babies have been born, couples have married and separated, and death has taken its toll. Every human advancement changes our world, and so does every backward step we take. Each time we win a victory or suffer a defeat, the result alters the conditions under which we live. Failure to realize this can lead to no end of trouble.

Divorce courts are overloaded with cases involving husbands and wives who forget that marriage is not a static affair, but a dynamic partnership, which will inevitably grow weaker unless nourished with constant care and attention.

Parents are amazed when their child runs away from home. They don't see how it could happen. In tragically extreme cases, when a youngster attempts to take his life, the distraught mother says, "I never believed anything like this was possible. I thought I knew my child better than this." Of course such surprise indicates how wrong we can be, when we forget that youngsters change, often profoundly, if neglected and deprived of the affection and guidance they need.

Even when you are unusually close to another individual, you cannot always be sure how he will react under all circumstances. About the only thing you can be certain of is the inevitability of the unexpected.

A computer expert was hired by a television network to compile statistics on audience preferences, correlate the data with a variety of proposed new programs, and then predict which shows would be a success. Despite the most meticulous research methods, only once was the computer correct in its projection of television programs that the public would like and dislike. Technical know-how cannot compensate for all the human variables.

No two situations are ever exactly alike, and every human being is a continually emerging personality, never the same from one day to the next. Any father who disregards this may complain bitterly that his children are acting crazily. What he really means is that he cannot depend on them to behave or believe as he has always assumed they would.

Down through the ages, the younger generation has tried to tell its elders, "We are not like you. We don't think as you do, and we don't cherish the same traditions." Whenever the argument has been voiced, it has largely been ignored by parents and teachers who felt they knew what was best for their children and also understood the adolescent's reasoning processes and emotions.

Juvenile upheavals now are causing many grown-ups to reconsider whether they really know at all what turns today's youngster on. All of a sudden we can't be sure how anyone reasons, or what he will decide to do.

The clergyman is confused about what the members of his congregation expect of him or the church or themselves.

Educators wonder how they can operate schools in a way to satisfy both their concepts and the demands of a new generation which doesn't conform as mothers and fathers used to do.

Thousands of business men annually go bankrupt by operating their firms on old-fashioned ideas. Customer needs change and unless those needs are met, the public will go elsewhere to buy.

Time after time an ambitious ruler has been too sure of himself and has misread his prophetic powers, concluding that a given action on his part would produce a predictable response from the head of another government, only to learn too late that he had pushed his country into a bloody and costly war. These endless conflicts have taken millions of lives and proved nothing but human unpredictability.

If you want to take anything for granted, believe in the unreliability of the past as a guide for the future. Our mistakes, tragedies, even our successes, only record what happened at other times. They

44

do not necessarily teach valid lessons for the future. Blind reliance on past experience can lead to disappointing and even disastrous conclusions. Certainty leads to over-confidence, carelessness, and failures. Think how much wiser it is to live each day with full appreciation that there may be something you need to know, something that has changed without coming to your attention. Try to evaluate each problem you face in terms of the present situation. Above all, remember that everyone you meet is a volatile, dynamic creature constantly revising his attitude, opinions and reactions.

You can never be certain that you know how anyone will react to a given situation. Your safest course is to listen, study, stay alert and sensitive to what is happening. It is the only wise and reasonably safe way to meet the challenges of each new day.

Ideas Have Miracle Power

"No army can withstand the strength of an idea whose time has come," said Victor Hugo.

Ideas have the power to ignite explosives, to mobilize nations for battle, or to build fantastic ships and bridges and skyscrapers.

An idea took seed in a man's mind centuries ago and sent him searching for new lands across a then unexplored and forbidding ocean.

The idea of human freedom as a God-given right impelled the prophet Moses, sparked a Renaissance and Reformation, gave meaning and courage to the leaders of the American Revolution.

Each idea must germinate like a seed in the warm soil. When it has been carefully fertilized and nurtured and its time has come, the idea will burst forth, breaking the bonds of earth that hold it, and all the armies in the world cannot contain it.

There is something sobering, almost frightening, about the volatile, explosive thoughts we carry around in our heads, carelessly tossing them out at the slightest provocation. Yet the ideas we treat so lightly have the capacity to create friendships or destroy understanding, to help or to hurt, to affect ourselves and the lives of others for better or for worse. An idea whose time has come is an extension of immortality itself; for a great thought can echo and re-echo from one generation to another, informing and inspiring, leading and guiding mankind to new heights of accomplishment and happiness.

The man with a good idea can literally change the course of the world. Keep it in mind. Respect those ideas you keep dreaming up. One of them, when it's time has come, may be the idea that makes you an unforgettable person.

The Lesson of the Dinosaur

Many of us are like what dinosaurs must have been——big and strong, endowed with single track minds and a dangerous inability to change with the times. To illustrate: one day a housewife and her husband were talking politics. Their viewpoints differed. Suddenly the wife yelled, "Don't say anything more. I've already got my mind made up and I don't want to change it."

This is quite common. We want very much to be right. We make up our minds and fight like blazes against changing or admitting that we are wrong. To confess a mistake in judgment embarrasses us so badly that we prefer to lie to ourselves and to others rather than openly facing up to an error and correcting it. Too often, we go through life holding tightly to our pet notions, regardless of how wrong or ridiculous they may be.

To many of us, problem-solving discussions are merely sessions for expressing our biased and prejudiced views on the matter at hand.

In other words, we do not use a discussion to learn but to "sell" our own firmly-held opinions and to resist others.

Therefore, when a group gets together to discuss a problem, there is too much tendency to disregard evidence and facts, and to accept only that which helps to fortify preconceived notions. Too often we are not seeking the correct answer but merely any answer that we think will sustain our point of view.

If we don't like what we see or hear, we are prone to discount it. What we fail to grasp, we are likely to disregard. We are comfortable only with what is familiar to us and favorable to our own attitude and opinions.

The speaker we applaud most loudly is the one who tells us something we already accept as true, not the spokesman who challenges us to accept a fresh thesis or theory. This kind of thinking stymies progress. To find meaningful solutions to problems, we must be willing to shed a concept if it is proved fallacious. In fact, we should be willing and anxious to discard our belief about a particular matter—if we are given a more believable alternative.

This is not simple or easy, for a better answer is not easily found or recognized, much less adopted. But it is necessary. To keep abreast of this fast-changing century, we will have to seek and accept new answers. We'll have to adapt to the discoveries and developments that, time and time again in recent years, have made obsolete and inadequate many of our assumptions about the world in which we live.

Animals that cannot adapt become extinct. This must not be the destiny of man. The dinosaur should be more than a museum curiosity. It should teach us all a valuable and sobering lesson: we must change with the times if we wish to stay alive and healthy and strong.

Keep Stretching Your Mind

The first time he saw the majestic Alps, Oliver Wendell Holmes was profoundly moved. He realized that he was viewing something so awesome and imposing that the experience would forever change his entire concept of the world and his place in it.

In discussing the episode later, he said, "Every now and then a man's mind is stretched by a new idea or sensation, and then shrinks back to its former dimensions. After looking at the Alps, I felt that my mind had been stretched beyond the limits of elasticity, and fitted so loosely on my old ideas of space that I had to spread those to fit it."

I wonder what Holmes would have said had he lived in this age when he could have watched and listened as three men traveled to the moon and back. The miraculous voyage of the astronauts affirmed to even the most skeptical that we live in an age when miracles can still happen, if we are willing to learn and believe and apply ourselves to the tasks we want to accomplish. Now, more than ever before, the key to our future, individually and as a nation, can be summed up in two words: adaptability and growth.

In a world where discoveries are continually upsetting our beliefs and assumptions, it is often a matter of survival itself to be able to learn new ways of thinking and doing things.

Yesterday's ultimate is almost invariably surpassed by record-breaking developments that challenge us to change our mind and our attitude if we expect to remain knowledgeable and capable of meeting our responsibilities.

Even when survival is not at stake, adapting to a changing world is necessary in order to capitalize on your opportunities. The really discouraging citizen in our midst is the person who prides himself on what I would call the flat-earth kind of thinking. Despite overwhelming evidence that he is wrong, such a person still is unwilling to alter his viewpoint or opinion.

James Russell Lowell must have had such stubborn souls in mind when he wrote, "The foolish and the dead alone never change their minds."

All through history there has been a competition waged between those who want to hold on to the dead hand of the past and to steer clear of entanglements with the mysterious unknown, and those who see the future as an adventure beckoning each of us to find new and superior ways of doing things.

It is a battle between those who think the pattern is set and those who know that mankind can create a better world if he will only try to stretch his mind and open his heart a little more each day.

Love

The Meaning of Love

Love is the most misused of all words. It may also be the most misunderstood. Love is like a weary talking horse which is called on to recite poetry, haul a wagonload of junk, run a race at Pimlico, perform in the circus ring, chase bad men in a western movie, and jump over the moon with Lady Godiva—all in the same day.

We hear that love is what makes the world go around, but what does it mean? We say that human beings *fall* in love, but if anything, love lifts us *up*. The fall comes when love departs!

We read that love is the greatest of all balms and the ultimate cure for mankind's ills, but we haven't succeeded in brewing any such elixir.

For most of us, love is an illusion. It's a fantasy, a Walter Mitty dream that we conjure to fit any one of a thousand different situations. A hearty eater loves food. A composer loves music. A child can love his mother. Mother may love to be alone, and father may love an argument. There are pleasure lovers, adventure lovers, sports lovers, and nature lovers, lovers of work and lovers of play. Some people love to hate, and others hate to love, and still others love to love.

Obviously, love means many things to many different people. It's such a convenient and useful word that it gets batted about like a tennis ball. And that reminds us, they play love games on a tennis court!

Love! What a beautiful, lyrical, inspiring, confusing, and at times maddening four letters. Think about this matter of love making the world go around: you and I know that the world operates despite the absence of love. For centuries this battered old globe has withstood all manner of mistreatment and still manages to smile with new life every springtime—so it must not exist on love but on hope and faith.

Consider now the proposition of a man and woman falling in love; that, too, is a myth perpetrated by the romanticists. What really happens, as everyone who has experienced it knows, is that two people find that they complement and desire one another. The attraction usually is a combination of physical and mental allurement. It is what Robert Frost called, "an irresistible desire to be irresistibly desired."

What we misconstrue as love, therefore, may be simply a reflection of self-adoration, a form of recognition and self-gratification. When we profess to love someone, we are expressing our own need for warmth and affection. Invariably, even a secret love, unspoken and unreturned, is played out fully on the stage of the mind to meet a purely personal need. Loved ones are dear to us because they bring us joy and make us feel important, wanted and necessary.

Even in affirming our love of God, we usually miss the mark, confusing love with awe, respect, fear, or worshipful adoration. Read what the Bible teaches of love, then compare it with the way we live; you will conclude, as I have, that we do not know how to associate God with love.

What then is the purpose of the poet's sonnets, the Biblical Psalms, the countless books and sermons and serenades that praise, exalt and glorify love?

American poet John Ciardi has pointed out that "love is the word used to label the sexual excitement of the young, the habituation of the middle-aged, and the mutual dependence of the old." And writer-editor Peter de Vries has ventured the opinion that "love's blindness consists oftener in seeing what is not there than in seeing what is."

How can we not be blinded by the prismatic qualities of love and the way we twist our interpretations of love into a multitude of incongruous shapes and forms? We hear of sacred love, erotic love, platonic love, and brotherly love; and we may conclude, as youngsters often do, that we can believe only what we personally feel.

What, for instance, is love of country? Is it to carry a rifle or to refuse? Is it to conform or to dissent? How much does love demand and how much does it permit? How deep and wide is love and what does it embrace? And what does it exclude?

When man is able to reconcile the many "loves" he bandies about so freely, perhaps he will discover a new meaning in life itself. When love becomes being and doing, rather than mere words, then we may begin to find what love is all about.

Meanwhile, the search goes on for answers; as man tries to invent a love that will meet his needs—a love he can feel and understand and breathe. Admittedly, it is a groping, awkward and clumsy search that has been going on for so many bloody and disappointing centuries, it is a miracle that so many still hunger for the dream.

Perhaps we are driven to determine the dimensions of love because there is in all of us a desperate longing to be better than we are, to cleanse and exalt ourselves, to stand on a higher pedestal and move a step nearer to immortality.

Anthropologist Ashley Montague calls man "the most extraordinary of all nature's performances: a most improbable creature, brash and bright, a spoiled brat, in fact—full of promise, only a small part of which has been realized."

Isn't love man's key to realize himself, to unlock the door to his limitless future? Love may yet explain to man his role in life, his relationship to other human beings, and his obligations to them and to God.

Although we do not yet grasp the essence of love, or know how to give and receive love gracefully, our efforts are deserving of some credit. We may yet find together what we have not discovered alone

—the realization of Antoine de Saint-Exupery that "love does not consist in gazing at each other but in looking outward together in the same direction."

Love to Be Loved

When a multimarried man applied at the courthouse for his seventh wedding license, the curious clerk asked why the applicant had failed so many times to make a go of matrimony. "Well, I keep looking for somebody who will truly love me," said the still-optimistic suitor. "Up till now I haven't found her, but maybe this will be the one."

There's something plaintive and pathetic about such a person. He keeps trying desperately to find someone to love him because he wants, above everything else, to be desired and needed.

Most human beings carry on similar searches for affection and approval, and our methods oftentimes are just as ineffective and illogical. Like so many hungry puppies, we parade around begging for a bone, hoping to be noticed, praying that someone will adore and protect us.

It is a mistake, though, to think that you can be lucky in love. Two individuals may be initially attracted to one another when meeting by chance; but if they wish to cultivate any kind of real, lasting relationship, it must be developed through daily demonstrations of consideration and concern. You cannot be a gambler at love and trust that good fortune will fill your life with joy. If you want someone to care for you, you must give that person good reasons to feel deeply about you.

Here again our methods are often awkward, revealing only too clearly that we want primarily to be loved rather than to give love to someone else. Consider, for instance, how much effort goes into buying love rather than earning it. In our neurotic compulsion to become the center of someone else's world we may spend a lot of money for flowers, perfumes, expensive clothing, and jewelry, hoping that these will be tangible evidence of our worthiness and desirability. This kind of generosity completely disregards the proverbial advice, "Love can neither be bought nor sold; its only price being love."

But giving love completely and unselfishly isn't easy, and so it is frequently bypassed. Instead, we substitute the token or the present. In a variety of ways, we try to barter our possessions for someone else's love and respect. This is one reason that many wealthy philanthropists give large sums of money for educational and cultural projects. I once asked an immensely rich man why he had endowed a particular school with so many of his millions. He answered quite frankly, "It makes me feel good. I get a lot of pleasure from knowing that the students and teachers love me and need my money."

At least he was being frank about his benevolence, but are we loved for the money we spend? Are we needed as much as we would like to assume? Many times we must think not, or why else would we continue so persistently to demonstrate our longing to be accepted, even to be enslaved by love's sweet tyranny? No people on earth want more to endear themselves to others than do Americans. Consequently, our government spends lavishly to win friends and influence other nations. It doesn't seem to matter that although our declared intentions are to bring about more peaceful relations among all peoples, our donations are often in the form of guns, planes, bombs, and warships. As suitors seeking love, we come bearing strange gifts!

Surely there are better ways to earn the trust and regard of people in other lands, just as there are more convincing ways to demonstrate our love for one another here at home. Why don't we try to prove that we understand and appreciate the real meaning of love by extending it to every person?

Nothing we could do would more quickly win the respect, the admiration, and even the love of the world's millions, than to see Americans walking, talking and working with each other on terms of true brotherhood.

Love surpasses knowledge and speaks louder than any orator. It can envelop mankind if it is alive in the heart of each individual. It must work its miracles by being transmitted rather than absorbed. If we do not love, we are nobody; by loving, we make ourselves somebody worthy of being loved.

Making Marriage Work

What's happening to the grand old institution of marriage? Is it doomed to extinction? It is apparent that one out of four marriages is breaking up, usually during the green years when both partners are young, impulsive and shortsighted. Divorces, however, can happen at any time, even among grandparents who have been married for decades. At any inning of the matrimonial game, one or both partners may decide to call it quits, resulting in more than 400,000 unions being dissolved every year.

As serious as this situation is—and I do not minimize the consequences of breaking up any marriage—it doesn't prove that matrimony is on the rocks or that the ceremony of exchanging vows of love and fidelity is a losing proposition.

More men and women are getting married today than ever before in history, not just in actual numbers but in percentages as well. A few years ago, nine out of ten adults could be counted on to walk to the altar together. Now it's 95 percent, and the figure keeps climbing.

Even when a marriage breaks up for one reason or another, two out of three women and three out of five men rather promptly remarry. If they were disillusioned about the whole business, they would hardly plunge back into the wedding pool so hastily. Marriage is still a vital and flourishing institution because millions believe in it despite its hazards and its failures.

Perhaps if we understood why husbands and wives call it quits we could prevent many future divorces. Our mobile, urban civilization has torn up the solid, fixed foundations of the old-fashioned marriages that used to be possible in quieter, less hectic times. If mama and papa weren't happy together, they still managed in most cases to stick it out for the sake of the children and to prevent gossip.

People are more liberated today and less likely to concern themselves with what the neighbors might say. Women have become independent; instead of putting up with an unhappy marriage, they are likely to seek a way out, even when children are involved. Men are more affluent and do not worry unduly about the initial expense of a divorce action or the subsequent alimony.

Many young people approach the responsibilities of marriage with such a casual attitude that they often become quickly disillusioned over minor disagreements and head prematurely for the divorce court.

Marriages can break up for a multitude of reasons. Selfishness, immaturity and incompatibility seem to be the primary causes. Despite the best advice of parents, clergymen, physicians, and all the marriage manuals, many couples still find themselves unable to live contentedly together. It is at least gratifying to know that they generally blame themselves, or one another, but rarely do they attack the sacred rites of matrimony.

Research into our rapidly rising divorce rate indicates that many marriages are doomed from the start because the husband and wife both insist on being right in every dispute. Obviously, when two people disagree, both can't prevail. The only satisfactory solution to such disputes is to declare a tie, then forgive and forget.

"If husbands and wives would make sure never to go to bed angry at one another, millions of marriages could be saved," says a psychiatrist friend. He adds that this means being willing to apologize with endearing words. Clamming up and refusing to continue an argument won't soothe any ruffled feelings, but it's quite difficult to remain angry at a loved one who is wise enough to say, "I'm sorry, dear. Please forgive me."

Another big factor in broken marriages is too much reckless talk. In recent years husbands and wives have been encouraged to speak out. "Express your emotions. Don't be inhibited," is the accepted advice for achieving satisfaction through verbal release. But it may just be one of the worst things you can do to a marriage. Getting angry and letting fly with your feelings may do irreparable damage to the most stable union.

"Anger is often more hurtful than the injury that caused it," goes a proverb worth noting by all wives and husbands. Instead of exploding and saying things that will later be regretted, it is far wiser to deal with marital disagreements on a more constructive and rational basis.

These pointers can help settle even the most pesky marital disputes.

1. Try to be considerate of the other's viewpoint. It always takes two to make an argument, and only by calmly looking at both sides of a question can you ever expect to resolve differences in a lucid and peaceful manner.

2. Bide your time. There's always a temptation to raise a question or start an argument too quickly. It's far wiser to wait. Hold your tongue and mull over the matter festering in your own mind. Is it really as serious as you first thought? Oftentimes a second consideration results in your dropping a matter before it becomes a cause of serious confrontation.

3. If a problem must be discussed, play fair. Don't name-call or make wild accusations. Keep your discussion zeroed in on the subject, not on your partner's faults or on what some third party might have said. Try to hold your voice down and your temper under control. If you receive a harsh verbal jab and resent it very much, don't yell or strike back blindly. Try to figure out what the accusation really signifies. Use your head, not your emotions.

4. Don't run away and hide, physically or figuratively. If you go silent, you will not correct any troubles, but only compound them. Nothing is more infuriating to a wife or a husband than trying to talk with a "dumb" partner. On the other hand, be smart enough to shut up and listen when you should.

5. Keep your talk on a rational plane. Try to hold back tears which are an unfair weapon, and never use physical force. Be gentle, compassionate and mindful of your manners. Your willingness to talk and your obvious affection will go a long way toward resolving the worst donnybrooks.

Remember always that honest differences can be adjudicated in marriages when there is genuine love, trust and respect. Marital problems are never too tough to work out for two persons who want a common solution rather than a stalemate. Where the desire exists, the answers can be found.

58

Loving Is Giving

An old epitaph reads: "What wee gave, wee have; what wee spent, wee had; what wee kept, wee lost." That sounds a bit like a riddle, doesn't it—giving away something and still having it, losing what we retain?

It also has been written that we only possess what we renounce, but as you reflect on this thought, what at first sounds like double-talk begins to reveal its deeper meaning.

Most of us go through life concentrating on the accumulation of possessions. Some of us save money or buy up real estate. We may collect coins, stamps or other souvenirs. Quite a few compulsive "string savers" latch onto anything that touches their hands. As a result, attics all over the country are spilling over with assorted junk, most of which will someday fuel a backyard bonfire.

People hold on to scores of useless articles because of emotional ties to the past. Most of us dread letting go of anything that relates us by memories to loved ones or happier, less-troubled days. After both my parents died, the small-town house in which they had spent most of their lives sat empty and unused. It was many months before my sister and I could accept the practical answer of selling the place so it could again come to life for another family and serve the purpose for which it was built.

We had been reluctant to part with something that mistakenly we had thought was ours. Oh, we had a deed all right, but that only provided legal protection. It didn't really mean that we owned anything as solid and firmly planted as a house. While our loved ones inhabited its rooms, we had a living relationship with it, for it was here that we had grown up and shared so much joy and affection. But that was all we had—only ties of devotion and memory—for it is impossible to own any material objects. What we may think we are buying, we are only leasing for a lifetime at most. When our days are done, we must relinquish our rights, even to the largest fortunes and the most luxurious estates; whereupon someone else picks up the caretaker and custodial duties.

So what can we truly possess? Perhaps only what we renounce. Think how you gain self-confidence when you succeed in casting off self-doubts and fear. Note how you prolong your life by giving up harmful habits.

Money which looks so enticing in big quantities is only worthless metal and paper, filling up shoe boxes and safe deposit vaults, unless it is released to go to work. The simplest way to lose a fortune is to bury it. There is absolutely nothing you can do with money that lies hidden somewhere. It is of no more value than a handful of rocks. If you want to possess your money, you must make sure to put it into someone else's hands.

The same holds true for whatever talent you possess. If you hoard it and hide it, never using or demonstrating your abilities for others, then you are bankrupt and don't know it. Whatever you clutch to yourself and refuse to share, you lose. For all purposes, your usefulness is dead unless you make it available to others. The person who plans to write a novel and never gets around to it never really has a book inside himself. If he truly possesses it, he must free himself of it just as a mother holds a baby only by giving it birth.

Indeed, the marvel of possessing what we renounce is most dramatically evident in our relationship with one another as friends, lovers and family members. "Love gives itself, but is not bought," said Longfellow, and in the giving, we receive all that we offer and more. The deeper our love for someone and the more completely we exhibit our unselfishness, the greater measure of affection will we receive as our bounty.

Parents have a natural desire to safeguard, protect and possess their children as long as possible. But those who are wisest try to prepare their youngster for the day when he can break the parental ties naturally and painlessly. By allowing their sons and daughters freedom to mature in a wholesome manner, learning to think and act and live for themselves, parents can still possess what they have relinquished. The emancipated son or daughter who is truly free returns parental love willingly, not from fear and not from a feeling of dependence. Any mother or father blessed with this devotion knows

60

best of all what it means to own and cherish what you have given away.

Of all the dramatic examples that might be cited to prove that we save only by spending, the most impressive is yourself. You are a transmitting agent, as are all humans. Life has meaning for you only when it has meaning for someone else. You live as you give, for in sharing yourself with others you receive in return the sustenance you need.

"Nothing truly can be termed my own, but what I make my own by using well," said the eighteenth century English divine, Conyers Middleton. "Those deeds of charity which we have done, shall stay forever with us; and that wealth which we have so bestowed, we only keep; the other is not ours."

Think of the many gifts you can present to others and gain a full measure of contentment and satisfaction in the process! Francis Maitland Balfour recommended: "The best thing to give your enemy is forgiveness; to an opponent, tolerance; to a friend, your heart; to your child, a good example; to a father, deference; to your mother, conduct that will make her proud of you; to yourself, respect; to all men, charity."

That impressive list is only a starter, but it illustrates a few of the ways you can earn priceless dividends by loving to give and giving to live.

Please Like Yourself

A person who dislikes himself is capable of doing the worst things in the world. One such unhappy husband went on a murderous rampage, shot seventeen persons, killed his wife, and then took his own life.

Tragedies like this cause shock, then dismay, and finally the realization that a great many murders in this country are committed not by persons who are basically mean or ugly, but rather by individuals who are sick unto death of themselves and the world in which they feel themselves trapped and imprisoned. Simply put, millions of men and women are their own worst enemies. They don't go around admitting it publicly, but their actions say it ever so clearly.

Hospitals are overcrowded with emotional misfits who can find no pleasure in life and no pride in themselves. They have fallen into deep depression because they feel spiritually and emotionally bankrupt, unworthy of staying alive. Psychiatrists are treating a record number of patients, firmly convinced that they are flunking out at the expense of others who are succeeding. Quite often their emotional outbursts reflect intense jealousy, envy and insecurity. John Steinbeck has declared, "If we could learn to like ourselves even a little, maybe our cruelties and angers might melt away. Maybe we would not have to hurt one another just to keep our ego chins above water."

Every human being was born with a marvelous conglomeration of aptitudes and abilities; it's shameful that we can't be more proud of ourselves. Have you ever noticed how happy a person is when he likes himself? His eyes sparkle, he smiles freely and feels wonderful. When you ask him a question, he responds cheerfully and without fear because he has self-confidence. He knows his capabilities and his limitations, and he has learned to live comfortably with both.

Contrast that with the unhappy individual who carries around an enormous inferiority complex as though it were a hundred-pound weight. His eyes are dull, his chin drawn in to his chest; and he feels as though he is developing or already nursing an ulcer. This is the miserable sufferer who has convinced himself that he is ugly, ignorant and severely handicapped. How could he ever expect to like himself or be satisfied with such an attitude?

But opinions can change—even personal opinions about oneself. You can learn to appreciate your many good qualities. You can look at yourself and see a number of attractive features. You can be sure that your mind is bright and sharp, otherwise you would not be concerned about yourself.

Count your virtues the way you are told to count your blessings.

Total all that you have going for you. You will see that you are much more fortunate than you realize.

Goethe once wrote: "If you would create something, you must be something." Recognize your own resistance to enlarging your life, and then do something about increasing your outlook and magnifying your accomplishments.

Work on your personal appearance. Try dressing more carefully and grooming yourself deliberately to get compliments. Cultivate your smile, keeping in mind that it requires no more effort to look pleasant than to frown. Wake up your sense of humor and share with those around you more laugh-filled moments. Tell yourself that people do like you and will like you even better if you will try harder to like them.

Above all, don't be frightened. It's highly unlikely that you have an enemy in the world. Everyone you meet is just as anxious to be greeted in a warm and friendly manner as are you. Remember, too, that if someone gives you the impression he is hostile or indifferent, he may only be responding to a similar attitude from you. Don't let that happen. Determine that you are going to care more for others and make them care more for you. Decide also that every day offers many more possibilities for happiness than for disappointment.

With this kind of positive approach, you're bound to start liking yourself better and learn what it means to have a contented mind.

What Is Man?

Man is a wonderful creature, a wise and silly, laughable, lovable hunk of humanity with an enormous amount of know-how about almost everything except himself.

Man is a paradox. He loves what he hates and glorifies what he fears. Man thinks fighting is stupid, but he uses it as his strongest method of persuasion. He deplores war as inhuman and monstrous, but he spends more money on buying the tools of war than he does for all his food, clothing and shelter. In fact, although man condemns killing as barbaric and thinks capital punishment is needlessly cruel, he continues to commit murders at an unprecedented rate in the home, on the highway and the battlefield.

Man is funny about his feelings toward his fellow man. He speaks, for instance, of loving his neighbor—but he hardly knows the names of the folks next door!

Man sings many songs about love, and listens to a lot of lectures about how to win friends, and boasts that he hasn't an enemy in the world. He then goes shopping for a gun, a burglar alarm, padlocks, and a book on self-protection!

Man hears all the time that he should get involved and he thinks it's a good idea, but he doesn't know where the action is. Man admires happy faces, smiles and laughter, but he's suspicious of anyone who looks too happy, too joyous or too pleased with himself.

Man boasts of his truthfulness; but he excuses little lies, white lies and diplomatic lies. Accuse man of being a thief and he is insulted; but let him stay overnight in a hotel room and he walks off with towels, clothes hangers and soap. Man is especially proud of being honest, but this doesn't cover such matters as income tax returns, golf scores and the excuses he makes up to cover his thoughtlessness and neglect.

Man says that his soul and spirit are of paramount importance, but he devotes most of his time and energies to pursuing material goals. Man is conscious of his power, but he feels powerless to control it. In fact, he frequently complains that he is an impotent digit in a world of impersonal numbers. This is a masochistic game that man plays, punishing himself, calling himself derogatory names; but let anyone else accuse him of being pitiful and unworthy, and he flies into a rage.

Man fancies that he needs adversity to keep himself alert and lean and strong, when what he really needs are loved ones to nourish his ego and warm his heart. Man hides in the corner with his fears when he wants to dance in the sunlight with his dreams. He clutches his mud pies like they were precious possessions, but he longs to throw them away and reach for a handful of stars.

Inconsistent as he is, this human being wants always to be a bigger and better person, nobler, kinder and wiser, neither slave nor master, but a free, emancipated man.

The Healing Power of Love

Comedian Bob Hope tells of a priceless ingredient that is used in treating injured Americans at military hospitals here at home and overseas. The essential medication, more important at times than miracle drugs or surgical skill, is love. You can see love and feel it in the devoted concern and attention given to every sick or wounded service man.

Love appears to work miracles in speeding an injured man's recovery because it is a special balm. Love can succeed where medical know-how sometimes fails. Love can touch minds in magical ways and mend mangled bodies, just as it can heal a broken heart. Anthropologist Ashley Montague doesn't know what the reasons may be, but he states flatly, "There is now sufficient evidence available from a variety of sources to prove beyond any question that love stands at the very center of the system of basic needs."

There's a public school in New York devoted exclusively to educating youngsters who are suffering from severe language and hearing handicaps. To reach and motivate these children, the teachers rely principally on love. Just as hospitalized soldiers respond to affectionate care, so do tykes in this school learn to hear, speak and write better when treated with loving kindness and patient forbearance.

"It is doubtlessly more important than any specialized training we give them," says the principal. "What they need most is love. They constantly crave the assurance that we care for them and want to help them improve."

Unfortunately, this is only one school in a nation where hundreds more are needed. Boys and girls by the thousands are growing up in homes that are almost totally lacking in love or proper supervision. Unless children are adequately cared for and disciplined during their early, critical years, irreparable harm can be done to their personalities and to their ability to function as complete, self-sufficient individuals.

All over the country today grown-up children are wandering around as examples of what happens when a person is denied the affection he needs as an infant and in early childhood. Unable to relate normally to others, the alienated adult goes from day to day as though walking through a dark, narrow tunnel. This kind of love-starved person is generally insensitive to the feelings of others, because his own feelings long ago became stunted and deformed. He does not look compassionately at others. He fails to hear or understand human needs, as one does when he has basked in the warmth of love and known the security of affectionate cooperation.

Botanists have even done research on the reactions of plant life to loving care. They found that endearing words seem to make flowers flourish. If it's true of plants, certainly there's every reason to be mindful of the powerful effect that love can have on encouraging and motivating human beings.

We all need to love and be loved, to care for one another more than we now do, and to communicate much more closely as interdependent, related human beings. There are countless ways that we can show our concern and devotion, especially in the loving care we give to the sick, the aged and the needy. Our love can be expressed through repeated acts of generosity and by the prompt, compassionate response we make to a cry for help, whether it comes from a friend, loved one or stranger.

Any city would rather have a million dedicated citizens giving a dollar apiece to a charity than receive a donation of a million dollars from one philanthropist. The gifts of many, even if small, provide evidence of individual loving kindness; and this is the ultimate answer to all of mankind's ills.

Greater by far than the gift of dollars is the individual gift of love. This costs nothing but it is worth a fortune. It is, in fact, priceless. "Love one human being purely and warmly, and you will love all," said the German novelist, Jean Paul Richter. If, indeed, each of us could love all as we love one, then misunderstandings could be erased and bitterness made only a memory. We would heal not only millions of the sick, sad and lonely, but the entire ailing world would find itself finally on the road to full and lasting recovery.

Responsibility

The Buck Stops with You

One of the Army's oldest and most interesting games is called Buck Passing. Ask an old-time soldier and he'll tell you that life can be reasonably simple and trouble-free if you can only learn to pass the buck to someone else. This simply means getting rid of your responsibilities and handing them to another party. The catch in this little game is that the buck sometimes comes back like a faithful, old hound dog. When that happens you suddenly realize that you can't pawn off certain obligations.

When I was in military service, I found that it was easy to route information away from your desk, but the buck-slip attached to the material was so designed that you could always find out where an item was, and who had seen it last. Buck Passing could only be a temporary relief at best, because it did not eliminate final accountability.

Life gives us chances to pass the buck. At least it seems to tempt us with such opportunities, but again, it's only a temporary means of escape. Inevitably, if you succumb to the temptation, you will regret it.

Children try the buck-passing game as a means of getting out of doing school or household chores. One youngster will tell another to do a task that he was assigned to do. When teacher or mother finds out about the buck-passing attempt, swift punishment follows.

Grown-ups who try to pass off their duties to someone else find that they too have to accept punishment when they are found out. If an individual persists in his buck-passing attempts, for a long time after he has been exposed, he has stamped himself as a weak, vacillating and undependable character—one who is unwilling to carry his rightful share of the load, or take blame for his decisions.

While he was president of the United States, Harry S Truman had a sign on his desk, reading: "The Buck Stops Here." In carrying out the heavy responsibilities of his office, President Truman had to make some decisions of awesome proportions. He was the man who gave the word to drop the first atomic bomb to end World War II. His was the voice that activated the multi-billion dollar Marshall plan, started the Berlin Air Lift, and sent troops into Korea to save the government of that beleaguered country.

Having made up his mind, the president defended his actions against all critics and never tried to shift the responsibility to anyone else. The buck stopped at the presidential desk. Because it did, the name of Truman will claim an important place in history.

Each of us might well ask ourselves if we're letting the buck stop or passing it on. Are you personally involved in projects to benefit your community, or have you passed that buck to others? What about the promises you made to yourself regarding your home, the family and your career? Are you doing what you should—or passing the buck?

If you can claim that the buck stops with you, then you deserve a salute as a master of your own destiny. A. J. Cronin once wrote, "The virtue of all achievement is victory over oneself. Those who know this victory can never know defeat." He was describing the kind of individual who says it, because he means it: "The Buck Stops Here."

Freedom and Responsibility

When the Declaration of Independence was adopted, it was with full knowledge that the authors and signers were taking a bold and revolutionary step. The desire for self-government was so strong, however, that the colonials involved were willing to risk their lives and their property in the bold venture. Their ultimate goal, of course, was not to destroy an old order but to build a new one, to conceive and create a nation in which all citizens would be free, and the words "liberty and democracy," would be a living reality. Much thought and deliberation went into the wording of the Constitution, and the Bill of Rights that followed, providing for a government of, by and for the people.

The founding fathers realized that the infant nation could exist and grow, not by accident, or at the whims of the individual, but by maintenance of order and respect for laws. Unfortunately, there are today some among us—including pockets of collegiate militants—who insist that our Constitution is antiquated, and our governmental and economic systems are inadequate. They insist, therefore, that the whole kaboodle should be junked. Some of the violent revisionists may be well-intentioned. We suspect that a number are not; but if we concern ourselves with those who are legitimately motivated to protest the present political and social order, we still must insist that they recognize the necessity of government by the rule of law; that they value the preservation of a society in which each man's property is respected and his life is secure.

To tolerate any other condition could only lead to anarchy. This may be the wish of a few, but the overwhelming majority of Americans from all walks of life want no part of such madness.

There are provisions for changing our laws, for reforming our universities, for correcting our urban and rural deficiencies—all in peaceful ways. And this is happening. One needs only look around him to see heartening evidence at this time of both public concern and public response to many of our urgent needs. Still no government has yet been designed that is perfect, and no society can ever expect to satisfy in its functions and performance what every citizen expects of it.

We do know that ours is a nation built on lofty ideals. If we are to make these principles more than a promise for our people, each citizen must contribute daily toward the growth and flowering of justice, equality and opportunity. Whether in the classroom or the courts, on the city streets, or elsewhere in America, we will enjoy only as much freedom as we are willing to share, preserve and protect.

The Pursuit of Responsibility

Maybe you saw the same show that I did, called *The Pursuit of Pleasure*. For an hour it described how idle and rebellious youngsters are slinking through the alleys and avenues of self-gratification. The program dealt not with conventional pastimes, hobbies or recreational outlets, but rather with the far-out and oftentimes bizarre methods that some youthful citizens are employing to get their "kicks" out of life.

One of the best known spokesmen for this group is Dr. Timothy Leary, the self-styled prophet and exponent of widespread use of LSD. He calmly explained that the members of his cult are seeking deeper, hidden meanings than they can get from living in and observing the world as most of us prefer to do. "You can't count on the members of this cult," he said, "to work for your corporation, or to serve in the military forces, or to show allegiance to the present political system." It sounds revolutionary, and it is, but it's a revolt with a dead end as its goal. It attacks what we all know is vulnerable, but it offers no solution—only a retreat from reality and responsibility.

By their disavowal of social, political, economic and religious standards and traditions, these rebels with a dubious cause are supposed to be pioneering a brave new world for mankind. They are really unhappy children pursuing drug-induced rainbows, while the world around them cries out for guidance, help and leadership.

Unwittingly they are promoting the cause of chaos and deadly anarchy. Think how utterly confused and helpless we would become if everyone elected to follow a completely hedonistic course, beholden to no one, respectful of no customs and recognizing no responsibilities.

Who would provide the food? Who would maintain our schools, hospitals, libraries? Who would keep our transportation systems, manufacturing plants, and public utilities operating? Whom could we depend on to concern himself with the simple but profound matter of human survival?

Somehow in watching the idle, young beatniks and their sleepy-eyed female companions playing games with destiny, it seemed dramatically evident to me that here were the lost and aimless sloths of the sixties, not merely disillusioned about an imperfect world, but selfishly indifferent to what they might do to help improve it.

Somehow they have not been taught, or have chosen to forget, that not everyone can be completely self-centered—not everyone can live for the exclusive salving of his own ego. The depressed and disillusioned are not justified in writing off all their fellow human beings just because they have heard too many lies, seen too much duplicity, and witnessed too much of madness and murder. Somewhere along the way even the lowliest of the animal order learns that he must share the world—and all of its faults and limitations—with other creatures, so that together they can exist.

If there is no real desire to survive, then the lemmings must be labeled for what they are; but if we are witnessing only the tantrums of emotional adolescents and hearing the prattle of the spiritually impoverished, we should patiently but persistently help them to realize the dark and dismal hole into which they have crawled, and from which they must start climbing toward the sunlight that defies all of their candle snuffers.

Above the pursuit of pleasure there still is—and always will be—the pursuit of responsibility, so that we can accept ourselves as worthy members of the human family.

Be a Booster

While driving through New England, a tourist was especially impressed with one small village where the buildings were all freshly painted, the grass was a bright emerald, and the people walked with a jaunty air that demonstrated their good health and exuberant spirits. The visitor stopped in a shop to find out more about the town.

"What is it that makes this village so unusual?" he inquired.

"It's the greatest place in the world," replied the smiling merchant. "I figure it's also about the healthiest place. The air, the water, the soil are all just about perfect."

As the visitor nodded, visibly impressed, the storekeeper continued, "When I came here, would you believe it? I was weak as a kitten. Couldn't say a word. Didn't have a tooth in my head and hardly any hair. I was so helpless I had to be lifted out of bed. But look at me now!"

"Well, this is a wonderful town," said the tourist. "How long have you been here?"

With a twinkle in his eye, the spry Yankee trader replied, "I was born here."

You have to credit such a man for his civic pride and his willingness to speak up for his hometown. He's a real booster, a solid citizen who believes that anything worth preserving should be actively supported.

There are women boosters, men boosters and even some juvenile boosters. They come in all sizes and shapes, and contribute their time and talents to thousands of different causes each year—everything from promoting the local beauty pageant to spearheading a college's multimillion-dollar building campaign.

The two things that boosters have in common are enthusiasm and dedication. They believe strongly in the causes they promote. Unlike the press agent or the professional funds solicitor, the booster collects no salary and works long hours because he loves people and wants to prove it with generous acts of kindness and charity.

I don't know where boosters find all of their energy, but it seems that the harder they work, the better they look and feel. One of these tireless volunteers is the vice-president of a bank, a man who had cancer and licked it with surgery. Every year he drives endless miles, making hundreds of speeches boosting one idea: go to your doctor for a medical checkup. His speeches have prompted thousands of people to have medical examinations, and in numerous cases, cancer has been detected and treated.

If you want to become a booster, your services will be welcomed. You can volunteer to work with a variety of splendid public service organizations. The Red Cross, the March of Dimes, the Easter Seal Society, and hundreds of other groups are constantly seeking helpers and will greet you with open arms, plus a list of jobs that need to be done. If you enjoy sports or civic improvement, you might become a booster for the neighborhood Little League baseball team or the town's clean-up, fix-up project. Boosters make excellent leaders in school, church and charity groups. They're always seeking ways to give assistance, raise funds, help the needy.

The best boosters are Samaritans. They really can't be happy unless they are doing good deeds. I think it's important to recognize this characteristic of the booster because it helps you to understand that there are men and women who get fun out of being helpful to others.

One of the biggest boosters I know is a little man, hardly five feet tall, named Joe Gerson. He is a booster for at least a dozen hospitals, schools, athletic clubs, and religious organizations. Every year Joe personally raises more than $100,000 for various charities. When I asked him why he did it, his answer was simple: "It makes me feel good. Besides, when I was a poor boy, I needed help from others to get a college education; I also was helped in finding my first job and getting a start in life. Now that I'm able, I like helping others the same way."

It has been said that the surest way to achieve happiness is to lose yourself in a cause greater than yourself. Sir James M. Barrie added, "Those who bring sunshine into the lives of others cannot keep it from themselves."

Aren't those good enough reasons for joining the ranks of the boosters? When you lose yourself in some noble cause, you promote yourself to new heights of happiness and contentment.

Idealism

It's a Small World

The Apollo astronauts looked down from more than 200,000 miles and saw a little round ball that was too minute to be full of ferment, too quiet and still to be wracked with unrest and war, too smooth and symmetrical to be warped with fear and indecision.

By miracles of scientific achievement that won the admiration of friends and foes alike, the United States succeeded in proving that man can literally escape from the troubles of the world. It is worth noting, though, that uppermost in the minds of the three brave men who rode to the moon was the thought of returning home—back to the good, green earth, to loved ones, to friends, to crowded streets and traffic jams, and all of the multitude of trials and tribulations that every earthling must bear.

The farther those three astronauts sailed away from the earth's gravitational pull and the deeper they flew into space, the more clearly were they able to see what is beautiful, noble and endearing about this globe we inhabit. If everyone could have a similar experience, perhaps we might be better able to understand how big are the evils we commit against one another and how small they make us appear in the vastness of the universe.

Why should the little creature man spend any of his precious moments making his life, or the lives of his neighbors, miserable? Why should any human demean himself when he is capable of being a giant, a Samaritan and a genius? If our schools and our industries can produce technicians and equipment capable of flying to other planets with unerring accuracy and dependability, then we also can produce volunteers with the will and the know-how to prevent war, eliminate disease, lick poverty, and overcome hunger.

It is within the capabilities of man to remove the obstructions that block sensible advancement, to erase the ugliness that blights so many communities, and to ease the suffering and sadness and adversity that beset so many lives.

Any social order that is able to build a bridge to the moon can also build bridges of human understanding and inspire men, women and children of all races and creeds to live in harmony and to use their immense technical knowledge for peaceful, humanitarian purposes.

As we move forward into a new age of chance and challenge, one resolution should be on every person's lips—a pledge to complain less and cooperate more in overcoming our common problems.

It's such a small world. The family of man, for all its four billions, is still a tiny tribe. Our astronauts saw this from afar. There's still time to profit from their observations and to make this planet a place of peaceful progress and unlimited opportunity.

No Time for Do-Nothings

"All that is necessary for the triumph of evil is for good men to do nothing." Edmund Burke sounded that warning two centuries ago. His advice is even more pertinent now because evil works in a much more sophisticated and insidious manner today; and innocent, good people can quickly be engulfed by ugly tyrants if they offer no resistance.

This raises the logical question, "What are the forces of evil that threaten us?" Two of the most dangerous are *ignorance* and *indifference*. When people do not know, and make no effort to find out what is happening in this world, they are easy prey for all kinds of predators. That's how incompetent officials get elected and manage to stay in office, despite glaring faults and shameful inefficiency.

It is the answer to the mismanagement that flourishes in so many public and private organizations. Ignorance and unconcern can be diagnosed as the root causes of most ills besetting our neighborhoods and communities, and the basic reason that we are plagued by so many national and even international disputes, cold wars and hot wars.

Where there is ignorance, there is misunderstanding of both motives and methods. Where knowledge is lacking, there is a related unawareness of the need for overcoming ignorance. The two go hand in hand. This is why it is so critically important that we encourage the greatest amount of unrestricted public reading, writing, listening, viewing, and discussion. "Freedom to know" must be protected by our laws and our courts, just as must our freedom to talk about matters that arouse our concern. The daughter of the late Joseph Stalin, now in America, has declared that she was finally impelled to leave her native land and to disavow allegiance to its Communist government, because she was not allowed to enjoy freedom of thought or expression. There must be millions of other people in Russia who would relish the opportunity to think and act as free men; but the forces of tyranny, which used ignorance and illiteracy to gain power in that nation, still maintain rigid state control of thought and speech. They achieve this by censoring the books that may be read and those that may be written, the broadcasts that may be aired, and subjects that may be taught or studied.

In this country, some people get impatient at times and suggest that we, too, should have more control of our channels of communication. As, for example, the absurd pronouncement by a high official in Georgia that we ought to have a big book-burning in the state. He should have known better. He should have known that neither he nor anyone else has the right to halt the spread of knowledge. Each American citizen must retain the inalienable right to decide for himself those books that he considers bad. And in the case of small children, the decision must rest in the hands of parents and trusted friends, not with the government or a censorship board.

To destroy books or ban information in wholesale fashion is comparable to immolating a person in order to remove a wart from his finger. Pray God, we will never become a nation controlled by censors, but instead will remain guardians of free minds and free expression. It is the only sound way to combat ignorance, illiteracy and apathy, and to make sure that men of good will do indeed triumph over the forces of evil.

Your Mission in Life

One day a visitor to an observatory remarked, after viewing the star-filled heavens, "It's plain to see that man is nothing but an infinitesimal dot in an infinite universe."

An astronomer, overhearing the comment, replied: "What you say may be so, but I hold to another viewpoint. It is true that man is an incredibly small dot in a limitless universe, but remember that man, among all the creatures, knows this. Furthermore, he is able to study and observe the universe. He is able to read and write about his observations. He is able to ponder and plan and actually take actions in concert with his fellow man to change the character of his world and his universe. This makes man something more than a lifeless, meaningless dot, doesn't it?"

Every person has a mission to grow from a tiny speck of protoplasm into a productive human being. Every one of us inherits a responsibility to leave this world a cleaner, better, finer place for our having lived in it and contributed to it. Eric Hoffer, the self-taught philosopher, is convinced that "Man is not only an unfinished animal, he is an unfinished man. His human uniqueness is something he has to achieve and preserve." Each of us is duty-bound to prove himself a strong link in the chain of enlightened progress.

Every nation has a similar mission to perform. Some countries acquit themselves nobly. Others engage in pillage and plunder, ignoring completely their role of responsibility to humanity and civilization. In its early history, America fulfilled its obligations as a helper for the homeless and a provider of sanctuary for the oppressed. In later years, this country became a defender of the democratic dream and an arsenal for those who opposed totalitarianism.

Since World War II, our storehouses have fed millions of the world's hungry. Our power has been deployed to help enslaved peoples. Our purposes have not always been understood, and our deeds at times may have lacked in wisdom or results what they were intended to accomplish; individuals, as well as nations, however, must accept the inevitability of criticism from some and opposition from others when prompted to meet a legitimate need, serve a noble cause, or uphold a sound principle.

With that in mind, this very day can become a starting point, a stepping-off place for many of us who have neglected doing our full duty toward our fellow man, our city, state, and nation. To paraphrase the words of St. Francis of Assisi:

> Where we have been selfish, we can prove ourselves more generous.
> Where we have been narrow-minded and prejudiced, we can open our eyes and our hearts.
> Where there is need, we can supply assistance.
> Where there is ignorance, we can shed the light of learning.
> Where there is despair, we can bring hope.

Where there is frustration, we can offer faith, understanding and love. We can accomplish all of this if we have the determination to do our duty.

The Bible speaks of love as "the fulfilling of the law." Nathaniel Hawthorne believed that man, unless frozen by selfishness and blinded by greed, could readily prove the truth of the Scriptures, for human nature "loves more readily than it hates."

It is up to everyone, then, to answer the stern voice of his heart and conscience. Lofty sentiments, you say, but can they be transformed into acts of goodness and kindness? That depends on how much our people want to translate dreams into realities. Franklin Roosevelt told an earlier generation of Americans they had "a rendezvous with destiny." Actually, this is the agony of every generation. Like it or not, we are designing tomorrow today.

If we truly care about our fellow man and the children who will succeed us, if our motivations are fair and just and our actions are honorable, our deeds will in time be accepted and appreciated.

What these deeds can mean to your own life is summed up in these words frequently quoted by Archbishop Fulton J. Sheen: "Sow an act and you reap a habit. Sow a habit and you reap a character. Sow a character and you reap a destiny."

Discipline

One More Round

They say that the great old-time fighter, James J. Corbett, had a philosophy about boxing. When you're taking a lot of blows and beginning to wonder whether you'll win or not, or even last out the bout, that's the time, as he used to put it, to "fight one more round."

Anybody who has ever played football knows what that means. During the early weeks of practice, the coach used to make us trot around the field to build up our wind. Around and around we'd go, jogging until we hated the football field and the coach, and were beginning to hate the whole idea of football itself. Then at the crucial moment, when we'd wonder if we shouldn't shed our uniforms and quit, we'd remind ourselves to keep jogging, to lift one leg and then another, to go for one more lap around that field.

Sure enough, we'd make it. Eventually the coach would blow his whistle, and we'd get to rest. Wonderful rest, with gobs of fresh air, and the chance to sit down on the cool, green grass, and feel pride in the fact that we hadn't quit. We had stayed for "one more round."

For most of us, life is pretty much like a football practice session, or a boxing match. Each day is another round of duties and obligations. It's easy to become apathetic or discouraged. We may wonder if it's really worth the effort to do a good job, to keep plugging away. "Who cares?" we ask—that's when we realize that *we* must care. Each person is responsible for his own destiny and must discipline his own life accordingly.

When he was in the White House, President Johnson is said to have told a reporter, "Whenever I feel I've done a good day's work, whenever I feel I've really accomplished something, I look at my desk. And then I go back to work, because I know I've only begun."

But is there any real value to be gained from going back to work and staying for one more round, sticking to the job?

Yes, there's plenty of evidence to prove that being willing to go one more round makes the crucial difference between losing and winning. The indelible footprints on the sands of time were pressed there by the work shoes of dedicated men and women who kept going.

Most of the games of life are won not by the strongest, fastest or most brilliant individuals, but by the pluggers—the hard workers who never quit, never say die, and always have enough pride and determination to go "one more round."

Remember to Forget

It's well-known that most of our emotional problems grow on us because we are unable to slough off worry and anxiety. We go to bed with a head full of problems, and we toss and turn through the night. Then we wake up the next morning with our head full of the same unresolved troubles. That's the way things are unless you've learned to give bad news the brushoff. I'm not suggesting that you should ignore serious responsibilities, but it isn't necessary to carry around your frustrations constantly. Much of what we remember should be forgotten. Certainly we would feel much better if we could wipe out a lot of unpleasant memories.

There is a knack that you can develop for giving dilemmas and disappointments only the amount of attention they deserve. In other words, treat a problem the same way you should treat an appointment with an unpleasant person. Accept calmly the fact that you must give up ten or twenty minutes in order to dispose of a disagreeable duty. Once you finish, dismiss the person and the problem from your mind.

We should adopt this attitude toward most of the perplexing matters that loom up to plague our lives. Learn to forget what isn't worth remembering. Learn to brush into a corner the resentments and worries that drain away your energy. Don't deprive yourself of the pleasure that a well-adjusted person should derive from work and play.

A successful salesman I know has mastered the art of remembering to forget. He is cheerful, full of spirit, adept at cultivating friends and influencing customers. He is healthy and happy because he locks his bad moments in his desk at night. "I never bother to carry home any of the insults, the rudeness, the ugly words, or scowling faces I have met," he says. Whatever was unpleasant, he forgets or files away, leaving his mind clear for optimistic thoughts, enriching memories and creative planning.

A good memory is often applauded as a wonderful asset. Equally important at times is the ability to forget!

Winning Arguments Without Arguing

Dale Carnegie declared that the best way to win an argument is not to get involved in it.

At first this may sound like cowardly advice. All of us find ourselves at times confronted by situations that demand that we take a stand. In speaking our mind we may well involve ourselves in a heated argument. What happens then is often not too pleasant or desirable. We can easily win an argument and lose a friendship, or worse yet, find that our contentious spirit has won us nothing but disillusionment and disappointment.

What then is the best way to approach someone when you have an honest difference of opinion to discuss?

No one method will work every time but you might consider airing your differing opinions in a unique manner. Instead of disagreeing, listen to the person opposing your viewpoint and try to repeat to him the essence of what he has just said.

Don't worry, and don't get the idea that this will brand you a weakling. Just have faith and echo what your fellow conversationalist is saying. Try to follow his reasoning. Remember now, you are not arguing, but neither are you conceding defeat. Not by any means.

This is a long-shot approach. You are gambling that your efforts to see matters from another's point of view will encourage that person to take a look at your viewpoint as well. Oftentimes, I have observed exactly that happen. Two persons locked in debate suddenly find themselves of one mind; and suddenly the air is clear, and harsh words are replaced by gentle complimentary remarks.

Why not give it a try? Don't argue. Just listen and feed back what you hear. Try hard to reflect accurately someone else's opinion. Then watch as that someone responds and, like slow magic, begins to understand and agree with you.

The Loser

What makes a loser?

A loser is someone who is convinced that he cannot win because the odds are stacked against him—so he fails to try. Then he stands on the sidelines and carps at the players who have chosen to get in the game.

A loser doesn't have any confidence in himself, and he resents anybody who appears self-assured. When he meets a confident person, he decides that he doesn't like him or trust him.

A loser operates on a set of negative rules, all of which are designed to prove why things can't be done. He can tell you all of the defects, dangers and undesirable features of any plan, but he can't offer one single suggestion for making it work.

A loser thinks that things are bad and getting worse rapidly, so he's inclined to do less today than he did yesterday and to predict that conditions will continue to deteriorate tomorrow.

A loser has no faith, so he is unable to wish or hope or dream about creating a better future for himself or for anyone else.

A loser thinks that good jobs and high salaries, special benefits and lavish retirements should be available to him—but he suspects that a conspiracy is denying him these advantages.

He also reasons that we used to have a good government and a strong country but no longer, and he believes that some terrible enemies are responsible; but when you ask him what he is doing to promote good government and a unified nation, he says, "That's the politician's job, not mine."

A loser thinks that new inventions cause more trouble than they are worth, and that people with original ideas are not only a nuisance but a menace as well.

A loser figures that people succeed in life either by luck or breaking the law. He doesn't realize that a man or a woman can be honestly motivated to work hard, to strive for definite goals, and to win.

A loser doesn't have much use for other people because he finds that too many of them are optimistic, smiling, kind, and happy; and all of this worries him. When he sees people in trouble, he isn't willing to help them because he is concerned only with his own troubles.

A loser specializes in complaints, gripes, arguments, excuses, and assumptions. He loses jobs, friends, opportunities, and loved ones.

A loser says that life is a rotten deal, and he spends all his time trying to prove it. He's the gloomiest, most cynical, suspicious defeatist in the world.

A loser is depressed, discouraged, afraid, and lonely. He doesn't admit it but he needs many things; and, above all, he needs enlightenment, understanding and love.

Don't let yourself be a loser. Think like a winner and enjoy a life full of hopes, dreams and satisfying accomplishments.

A Challenge to Youth

"Ask the young; they know everything," it's been said. Alarmists have always regarded the rising generation as a falling one; and youth, in turn, has felt that the older generation was impotent and indifferent.

"Young men have a passion for regarding their elders as senile," declared Henry Adams. In youth, everything may matter too much; and as we grow older, things may not matter enough. So a gulf exists between the young and the no-longer young, a credibility and communication gap that has plagued all civilizations. Egyptian Pharaohs issued proclamations denouncing wild and reckless youngsters who had no thought for the future and no respect for the present.

In the early days of his presidency, Franklin D. Roosevelt spoke about the restless, critical, challenging temper of youth: "Flaming youth has become a flaming question. And youth comes to us wanting to know what we may propose to do about a society that hurts so many of them."

Baffled parents, educators and politicians have been wrestling with student protesters for centuries. The problem is still a vexing one, for it remains unresolved. Perhaps it will always be this way, as young people test their ideas and ideals against the hard rocks of reality. The young do not believe in such words as "impossible," "impractical" or "unreasonable." Armed with the confidence of tender years and great passion, they march out to break a world that is not to their liking. And they are more brash and militant today than anyone can remember, demonstrating defiance of authorities and traditions in dozens of countries.

Even Fidel Castro—who was once considered by many to be the idol of the campus militants—has gone on the air to denounce young Cubans for burning flags, vandalizing and destroying schools, and even desecrating poster pictures of the late Ché Guevara.

The revolt of the adolescents is, indeed, a matter of concern to both democratic and totalitarian nations. It appears to be a world-wide movement of sorts against any established order. One of the young men who proved to be most militant and vocal at both Columbia University and later at the Democratic Convention in Chicago told newsmen he was too much of an extremist to be called a Communist.

A college president with whom I talked recently labels the most fanatic of the dissenters "a new breed of anarchists." They appear intent on destroying the old order in order to be the dominant force in a new state of disorder.

There are campus rebels who freely admit they have no blueprint for improving what they dislike, only a battle plan for crushing what now exists. It has been suggested by more than one psychiatrist that the most destructive of the militants may be emotionally unstable and in need of treatment. Certainly many of the most outspoken and ill-mannered demonstrate rather clearly that they are anxious only to have power and notoriety. They have learned that by acting as bullies they can intimidate a certain number of peaceful teachers, students and administrators.

I am not suggesting that schools and educators are fault-free.

There is ample justification for student complaints, unhappiness and, in some cases, even militant protest. Most of us well remember that schools do have some ignorant teachers, unfair practices, needless rules, and ridiculous restrictions. Like all other organizations, our schools and our teaching methods could be improved, and should be, to become ever more humanitarian, realistic and inspiring. Unfortunately, protesters don't always want to improve, but to punish. Student mobsters who ransacked a Canadian university's computer center wanted to wreck and destroy, not to reform or improve.

It would seem relatively easy to spot the few who are completely unreasonable and take measures to contain their actions; but, unhappily, a sizeable number of other students—less militant, perhaps even anxious to do what is right—have given sympathetic support to some of the most outrageous acts of insurrection.

When challenged by rebel leaders to choose between "heroic" student freedom and villainous administrative dictatorship, some well-intentioned students have thrown common sense and caution aside and plunged into the confrontation, making it bigger and more difficult to resolve.

Actually, there is no sharp line of right and wrong, as the protesters insist. Most educators want to operate and teach in schools that are places of free thought and free speech, with a minimum of restrictions on the way the students live, think and talk; but it is foolish to believe that any organization, system or social order can operate without reasonable regulations and limitations that prevent order from disintegrating into chaos.

I cannot believe that the vast majority of youngsters in the high schools and colleges of the nation do not realize this. Nearly everyone learns at an early age—from parents, brothers and sisters—that if you practice violent insurrection and trample on the rights of others, you must be punished and restrained.

The academic deficiencies of America cannot be corrected now or ever by tearing down the halls of learning. Students who dislike certain professors are not necessarily qualified to select better ones. Young critics who can draw up a long list of grievances might find it enlightening and an exercise in self-control to draw up an equally long list of their personal responsibilities.

Many students, millions, in fact, are serious, sober and responsible citizens, aware that whatever we buy, we must pay for. I watched former Vice-President Hubert Humphrey conducting a class at Macalester College where he is now a professor. Most of his students appeared to be bright, young men and women, concerned about the ills of our society, particularly our schools, and willing to do whatever they could to bring about beneficial reforms. There were a few in the classroom, however, who sounded as though they could not accept the avenue of peaceful change.

To them Humphrey calmly offered a choice: work to make better what is admittedly imperfect; or risk destroying your government, your social order and your liberties, imperfect as all three may be. I'm not sure that some of the angriest young rebels have thought much about the world they will inhabit in the coming years, but if they have any desire to make democracy live, they must remember one thing: you cannot kill the tree of freedom and still expect to stand under its sheltering arms.

For every citizen, regardless of his age, this is the choice and the challenge.

Sensitivity

Sharpen Up Your Sensitivity

Friends and foes of General Robert E. Lee marveled at his sensitivity. He seemed to possess a unique power for analyzing what his opponents would do under a given set of circumstances and then he would devise a counteroffensive to take advantage of the situation.

He also displayed sensitivity in his reactions to the wants and needs of his own men. Because of his empathy, he became deeply involved emotionally in the hunger and hardships they endured, and he suffered along with them.

Because General Lee was able to share so intimately in both the triumphs and troubles of his soldiers, he was extremely effective in leading his troops and motivating them to serve and sacrifice, above and beyond the call of duty.

His personality was akin to that of Saint Francis de Sales who observed, "Nothing is so strong as gentleness; nothing so gentle as real strength."

You may never become famous as a general or leader of men, but you can still win praise and promotions by sharpening up and displaying this same insight and awareness. William Wordsworth reminded us:

> That best portion of a good man's life,—
> His little, nameless, unremembered acts
> Of kindness and of love.

Sensitivity grows from your convictions, from having principles and objectives that are vitally important to you. Whatever is really significant in your life will almost invariably be what you are concerned about nourishing and protecting.

In many ways sensitivity is closely related to pride. The more strongly you feel about yourself and your personal responsibilities, the greater will be your ego and the more tender your feelings.

General Charles DeGaulle presented a constant challenge to Allied military leaders during and after World War II, because he was tremendously proud and inordinately sensitive. The slightest gesture or word would sometimes cause this vain man to exhibit harsh resentment of what he considered an insult; yet because he was so sensitive, DeGaulle demonstrated remarkable ability to understand the emotional needs of the French people and to lead them from despair to renewed strength and confidence.

Sensitivity must be practiced constantly if it is to be effective. It is a fragile, delicate probing device that tells us how someone feels and how he will probably react. It is also a messenger that advises a proper course of action.

The sensitive person knows what to believe when others are in doubt. He remembers when everyone else may have forgotten. He rejoices in someone's good fortune and sympathizes sincerely with another's misfortune. Sensitivity is a sixth-sense that alerts us when to say something and when to keep quiet. It is the little reminder bell that tells you to be courageous in times of crisis, and cautious in moments of peril.

Above all, sensitivity is the best device we have for maintaining a proper balance between too much and too little. Some call this common sense. Others may refer to it as good judgment or insight. I consider sensitivity to be a nobler virtue. It is the ability to use your judgment in a compassionate manner, so that your decisions are not only logical, but often are inspiring. This is the magical power of sensitivity.

Join the Golden Rule Club

Getting along with people is both a science and an art. Scientifically, it requires that you study human behavior and gauge your actions accordingly. As an art, winning and keeping the confidence and affection of others demands that you have a genuine interest in human beings and a warm regard for their feelings. I've drawn up a list of do's and don't's that may help anyone who wants to be well-liked, trusted and highly regarded. You might check to see how you rate:

1. *Do* practice thoughtfulness and courtesy. A small favor done at the right time is one of life's most endearing compliments, especially if you offer it as a complete surprise to the recipient.

2. *Don't* offer advice to another individual unless you are in a position where you have an obligation to be helpful. Among the world's least popular persons is the one who specializes in telling others how to dress, what to buy and where to buy it, what to eat, and how to decorate the house.

3. *Don't* gossip. When you hear something uncomplimentary about another person, forget it. If the news is big and bad, it will get around quickly enough without your assistance. Even the most innocent are sometimes suspected of carrying tales. The best insurance against being wrongly accused of such behavior is to make a habit of never indulging in the gossip habit. The character assassin plays a very dangerous game. In taking pot shots at others, he sets himself up as a big target and invariably gets hit with plenty of the same ammunition he uses against his victims.

(My mother never listened to unflattering talk about other people. The moment someone would start to tell her some juicy gossip, Mom would raise her hand and say, "I'd rather not hear it. If what you're going to tell me is untrue, it shouldn't be repeated. And if it is true, it's none of my business." That doubtlessly saved my mother many hours of precious time which she was able to devote to her flower garden, but it also endeared her to everyone in our home town. I recall distinctly that the most notorious gossip in the town, who chopped up just about everybody's reputation, loved my mother deeply and called her an angel.)

4. *Don't* take advantage of another person's time, talent or property. This alienates more people and erodes more friendships than any other thing. I'm not suggesting that you should hide away from people and refuse to be friendly. I do recommend, however, that you visit the same neighbors and relatives only occasionally, and even then it's much better to do it on a preplanned basis rather than to drop in unexpectedly. Similarly, don't constantly telephone even your dearest friend just for the purpose of idle chatter. An occasional call is certainly in order, but it should be kept to a reasonable length of time.

(One of the prime offenders about imposing on someone else's time is the neurotic who seems always to need a shoulder to cry on. Often such a person complains of being ill, but it's obvious that whatever ailments she suffers from have had no damaging effects on her power of speech. Another nuisance is the fellow who never runs out of problems that he wishes to discuss. It never enters this fellow's mind that many of the dilemmas he deliberates about and explains in nauseating detail are actually trivial and inconsequential matters, undeserving of his great concern and certainly not important enough to justify asking someone else to consider. A special pain in the neck is the borrower who helps himself to your belongings, sometimes with your knowledge and sometimes without. Even if he returns what he borrows—and frequently he does not—this person is one you'd be happier not knowing.)

5. *Don't* force your opinions on others. There is a time and a place for expressing your views on both major and minor issues. I heartily recommend that you sound off at the right time and the right place; but it is rarely ever advisable to seek out another individual—friend or foe—to volunteer your unsolicited, pet ideas or peeves.

(If you are asked for an opinion, and you have reason to believe that what you think will be listened to with interest and respect, by all means reply. Be honest and sincere. Tell what you think, and try to make clear why you believe as you do. When your opinion is based on substantiated facts, say so, for that is often helpful information.

You need not be squeamish about leveling with someone when you have been requested to do so. If your thoughts are welcomed and considered helpful, you will be asked again. If not, the person who approached you will still think highly of you for your frankness. Even in responding to a direct request for an opinion, it is wise to answer only what was asked for. Extended talk tends to sound didactic, smug and tiresome. Besides, no one listens to or appreciates a long, drawn-out explanation.)

6. *Do* try to be sensitive to the feelings of others. I know a few rare and wonderful persons who seem instinctively to know what needs to be said and done in any situation. Congratulations, if you are endowed with this rare ability! If not, take heart from knowing that you can learn a great deal about getting along successfully with people just by observing what pleases others. Remember also that you may be your own best teacher. Just try to ask yourself repeatedly, "What would be the correct thing to do?" "How would I feel if things were reversed?" In short, treat others as you would like to be treated. It's a golden rule that still works like a charm!

Try a Little Tenderness

"You have not converted a man because you have silenced him." John Morley wrote those words years ago to remind us of the utter futility of trying to coerce someone into an agreement. You may force a person into saying yes, but you cannot be sure he means it.

Sometimes a wife will harangue her husband so loudly and so long that he will agree to anything. An irate mother may fuss at her child and then conclude that the youngster understands and agrees with what she has said. Actually he may disagree completely but be afraid to say so.

Have you ever been stopped by an angry policeman and given a lecture for speeding? If so, you know what it means to sit quietly and passively, even when you are convinced that you were driving within the legal limits. Although you are discreetly silent in the face of authority, it doesn't mean that you have been persuaded.

I once played football for a temperamental and excitable coach who frequently would try to bully his players into making a greater effort to win. The more he yelled and threatened, the more we recoiled and rebelled inwardly. Our silence should have told him something, if he had been more sensitive; but he mistakenly thought we were listening respectfully and with great attention. You may be sure we won very few games under his questionable leadership.

It has long been believed by many old-time soldiers that you can break a man and then remake him into a real fighter. In fact, one of the commonest forms of hazing in military camps is to berate a neophyte unmercifully and forbid him to answer back with anything more than, "Yes, sir," or "No, sir." Having experienced this kind of treatment as an officer candidate some years ago, I found it not only distasteful but of dubious value. Anyone who has been browbeaten, humiliated and bullied into meek submission is not likely to bounce back with joyous enthusiasm when the pressure is turned off.

Sometimes ghetto dwellers who have achieved some degree of freedom will bedevil police by showing resentment rather than pleasure at their liberation.

If you have been mistreated, you doubtlessly remember well the one who abused you. I doubt that you hold any warm or tender feelings for your tormentor, even if years have gone by since the unpleasantness. Most of us find that kind of humiliation hard to forget.

Anyone who has been forced to obey, submit or be silent might understandably comply to avoid prolonged suffering. Members of the captured Navy ship, *Pueblo,* explained to a Court of Inquiry how they admitted guilt to their tormentors for offenses they did not commit in order to escape continued punishment. Compliance sometimes means only that we are submitting but not surrendering.

We can be convinced and we can convince others only where respect and believability exists. If you want someone to agree with you, you must win his confidence, his mind and his heart. So forget about force, and try a little tender persuasion.

The Right to Privacy

Like the whooping crane and the passenger pigeon, privacy is about to disappear from the American scene. As we move into closely packed cities and our lives become intertwined, precious privacy—which Emerson considered the stern friend of genius, and Gibbon loved better than friends—becomes harder than ever to find and enjoy.

Everybody now seems to be in the spotlight or striving to get there. "Smile, you're on camera," is more true than we sometimes realize. You can't find much solitude in a noisy crowd or a traffic jam, and that's where we spend an inordinate amount of our time.

The gentle, peaceful kind of privacy that you read about in books, or that you may once have known somewhere on a farm or in a small town, seems almost to be an imaginary world that never really existed. It has been replaced by a great deal of sound and fury, signifying nothing more profoundly than irritation and frayed nerves.

We can understand and accept with good grace the necessary noises of our age. Wherever millions of people turn millions of wheels and trip millions of hammers, they're bound to make a lot of noise. But there is much additional clanking that goes on in the city unnecessarily. Together we comprise a strident and discordant chorus, finding too many matters to argue and yell about. Think of all the horns, bells, sirens, shrieks, and gunshots that could be lessened or eliminated if we really tried.

Without acoustical treatment, most offices and dining rooms would reverberate like subway tunnels when the trains go rattling by, simply because human beings talk too loudly and far too much. Our emphasis on loudness and confusion brings to mind Mark Twain's comment: "Noise proves nothing. Often a hen who has merely laid an egg cackles as if she had laid an asteroid."

Our trouble is not limited to din and decibels, however, for it goes much deeper. We are a people afraid to be alone. So we congregate by hundreds and thousands, sacrificing peace and quiet, to make certain that we will feel security in numbers. Ours is a deliberate effort to escape privacy; and in the process we generate for ourselves headaches, confusion, unhappiness, and emotional turmoil that make millions of lives wretchedly unhappy.

We pretend to be busily sophisticated but we are only noisily naïve, trying to scare away our fears with myriad noises, much as natives in the jungle might beat on drums to scare away evil spirits.

A solitary figure sitting silently in the darkness should be an inspiring sight, but most gregarious Americans would think initially that the scene depicted loneliness and sadness. They would be attracted but apprehensive; yet, we need more of the priceless privacy that can be found in a quiet library stocked with good books.

We need the privacy that a family discovers when it closes the front door at night and gathers around a cozy fire in the den to read, chat or listen to good music. We need the privacy that two persons seek when they drive to the top of a windswept hill or stroll along a deserted beach at sundown, and the world seems to have put aside its anger and its frayed nerves.

There's a special kind of privacy that cannot be found behind solid walls or locked doors, or enjoyed in the company of a friend or loved one. It's the privacy that exists in the sanctuary of the mind. There, in silent reflection, we can straighten out thoughts that have been knocked askew, while nourishing our imagination and refreshing our spirits.

"What a strange power there is in silence!" wrote Emerson. "How many resolutions are formed, how many sublime conquests effected, during that pause when lips are closed and the soul secretly feels the eye of her Maker upon her!"

Yes, privacy can be restorative and pacifying. I am quite sure it is a basic need that some have learned to deny themselves, in the same way that a person may deprive himself of much-needed sleep. But man requires privacy and he must have a degree of aloneness to maintain sanity in his life. "How gracious, how benign is Solitude," wrote Wordsworth. Our planning for the future should give priority to privacy. If possible, there should be a "private" room in every house, a time for privacy in the business day, an hour of privacy for the student—in short, a premium on moments for meditation and places of retreat.

We will have to remember, however, that just as we share the confusion of this quarrelsome planet, so must we share whatever privacy we can provide. The less solitude there is available to us, the more dear it will become; and the greater it will be prized by all who seek the balm of isolation.

So the right of privacy—like all rights in a civilized and democratic society—requires of those who would claim it that they fairly and freely grant the same right to every other citizen.

How Prejudiced Are You?

Prejudice is like the TB germ. We all have a certain amount inside us. It lies quiet and dormant in most persons unless an occasion arises to trigger the multiplication process. As our emotional fever grows, so does our prejudice. Suddenly we aren't thinking rationally or talking fairly. We've been overcome by the germs of prejudice.

When an entire community becomes infected, this kind of hatred can assume epidemic proportions. It did in Germany under Hitler. It has run rampant through American communities, resulting in witch hunts, massacres and lynching parties. Prejudice has fired up howling mobs of book burners, church bombers, rioters, looters, super-patriots, and master-race theorists.

Generally, though, prejudice works quietly in its early stages. In fact, by the time it has completely deranged someone's mind or worked its ugly damage on a group of people, it is no longer recognized as prejudice. Then it is spoken of as insanity, ugly violence, irresponsible militancy, or extremism; but if you look deeply enough into the machinations of the troublemaker, you will find that his fanaticism has developed from a seedbed of prejudice, with all of its related suspicions and ignorant misconceptions.

Voltaire called prejudice "the reason of fools," and Hazlitt termed it, "the child of ignorance." These are gentle words that fail to come to grips with the meanness and danger that this sickness really represents.

Lord Francis Jeffrey, the Scottish jurist, was closer to the point when he advised: "Beware of prejudices. They are like rats, and men's minds are like traps; prejudices get in easily, but it is doubtful if they ever get out."

Sad but true—the bigot does not hold warped opinions; his opinions hold him in a vise-like grip and in many cases enslave him for life. Prejudice works in a variety of insidious ways. It causes the diseased mind to conjure imaginary wrongs, to strangle truth, to overpower reason, and to trample on human rights and dignity. Prejudice makes strong men irresponsible and weak men dangerous. Surreptitious and devious as it frequently is, prejudice loves to pass itself off as reasonable and rational opinion. The most self-righteous spokesman is sometimes the greatest bigot. He may pose as a great defender of his country, protector of his family, and promoter of the general welfare; but when you analyze what he says sometimes in public, more often privately, you begin to see that this is no honorable person at all, but an illiberal, contemptuous sadist who is proud of the stereotypes he collected as a child and which he still uses to classify and judge human beings.

Edmund Burke noted many years ago: "Instead of casting away our old prejudices, we cherish them to a very considerable degree and, more shame to ourselves, we cherish them because they are prejudices; and the longer they have lasted the more we cherish them."

It's disturbing to realize that anything as loathsome as prejudice should be a source of satisfaction to anyone, but you need only read the propaganda sheets of various hate organizations to understand how twisted minds can become.

To the person of conscience and goodwill, nothing should be more sickening than the sound of a malicious voice. But how do we know that we aren't all guilty at times of spreading damaging rumors, casting aspersions, dropping remarks that contribute to the spread of distrust and disunion?

There's a device you can use to test your own vulnerability to the virus of prejudice. Any time you feel the urge to speak disparagingly of someone, ask yourself why you want to do it. Go a step further and see if you have any verifiable facts with which to justify the charges you are tempted to make.

Prejudice shows itself in many ways, especially in harmful attacks made against a group of people. The criticism may be somewhat veiled, but its intention is to cause hurt to an entire class, race or religion. Yet we know in our minds and hearts that no individual can rightly be held accountable for an entire group, and certainly no group should be pilloried for the indiscretions of a single person.

Each human being deserves the right to be judged on his own merits and criticized or complimented on the basis of what he has done, or failed to do. His race, faith or social status should not enter into any consideration of the calibre of work he does or evaluation of his worth.

Notice, however, how often you will find a spokesman or a writer referring to an individual whom he obviously dislikes, as being of a particular religion or race. There are men and women who cannot resist the compulsion to claim superiority over another individual, or an entire class of persons. La Rochefoucauld in his *Maxims* explained, "If we were without faults, we should not take so much pleasure in remarking them in others."

Next time you become dissatisfied with someone's actions or attitude, ask yourself precisely why you are unhappy. Try to pin down the real cause of your displeasure. Are you dwelling on something that is wrong and can be corrected, or is it only your dislike of another individual? Is the real problem inside your mind where the prejudice virus lurks and dominates your thoughts and feelings?

Is malevolence at work, expressing itself in dislike for yourself and resentment of someone else? The only thing in God's world that we should be prejudiced against is prejudice itself. There is no excuse for showing an individual any less respect than you want for yourself. If you are truly respectful of another person's rights, then you will refrain from speaking of him as an inferior being and try to immunize yourself against vindicative impulses and stereotyped thinking.

A teen-ager will tell you that not all youngsters should be condemned as irresponsible because of the wild antics of a few. The college student who is peacefully studying and attending classes resents being called a wild-eyed revolutionary simply because there are a few such malcontents on campus. The policeman who does his duty conscientiously and well doesn't want to be held accountable for someone else's police brutality.

Each individual wants to be judged on his own, not stuck into a convenient group and given a label. Everyone feels the need to be dealt with as a very special person and to be considered on his own merits. How strange it is that we can recognize this so clearly within ourselves and yet not see the same need in others.

Instead, we constantly think in stereotypes. We consistently size up persons, favorably or unfavorably, on such unreliable evidence as size, weight, height, hair color, clothing, speech, and physical handicaps. It is not uncommon for an individual to be judged by where he lives, the school he attended and whom he knows. It should be obvious that such methods of judgment are faulty and unfair. Surely you don't want to be judged that way, so why should you expect anyone else to willingly accept this kind of treatment?

The best way to combat prejudice is to recognize how it embitters the lives of those it infects and harms those it attacks. Put yourself in the shoes of each person you meet; and remember that here is another human being who deserves to be understood, respected and appreciated. Don't waste your time fearing and resenting "people." Get to know and like "individuals," and see how much happier your days will be!

Seeing in the Dark

A darkness descended upon the land. And it was night. And the sun did not rise. And mysteriously the lights did not glow. There was no illumination. Men and women were so afraid they huddled together in the blackness, shivering and moaning and despairing of their lives until gradually they learned to exist this way.

No one knew when day ended or evening began for the sky was always purple-black; and there was no sunlight, no moonlight, no lamps, not even a candle to pierce the darkness.

So people were like moles, blind and unable to see one another; and they were reduced to communicating by words and by touching one another. Many beliefs and customs and mores were quickly changed or forgotten, for they no longer had significance or usefulness. Beauty and ugliness became one and the same, and boundaries and barriers lost their meaning. Since barbed wire could entangle a friend as quickly as a foe, no one tried to trap or impale anyone else.

Actually there were no enemies, for the people were reduced to equal strength, or universal impotence, and found comfort in clinging together, sharing truths and troubles without embarrassment or shame —brothers in blackness.

And as they huddled in the common darkness that hid all differences from their eyes, they could not tell the color of one another's skin, or the angle of another's eyes or the cut of anyone's clothes. They were pitiful pilgrims holding hands, praying together in the purple permanence of night.

And the older ones who remembered most about the past saw at last in their blindness what they could not see in the brightest sunlight. At last they could see inside one another's minds and hearts; and there they found no social classes, no races, no superior creed— only humble humans trying to merit the trust and friendship of their fellow beings and the merciful forgiveness of God.

Achievement

You Must Climb Mountains

Man is a natural mountain climber, not because he likes to climb but because he needs ever so often to win a battle.

When astronaut Walter Schirra, Jr., was asked why we should send men to the moon, he answered simply, "Because we can do it." The long-range benefit of moon-probing he would leave to others. For Schirra, merely proving that man can get there is a laudable objective.

This is becoming perhaps the most valid of all reasons to give for undertaking a tough job and doing it in a superior manner. Don't shirk your responsibility or shy away from an opportunity. Do it because you can. You will win much more in the doing than you may realize.

Christopher Columbus crossed the ocean because he was certain he could. It was a voyage that unlocked the door to a new world. Expeditions to the moon, and eventually to more distant planets, could also reveal frontiers that do not now exist for us. The man

107

who climbs a mountain does more than satisfy himself of his capabilities. He motivates others to become mountain climbers.

The astronauts who blasted off to the moon caused millions to look upward together in awe and admiration. Their feat had a remarkable unifying effect on this nation, and people all over the world rejoiced at their noble achievement.

So clearly, when we do something tough and worthwhile—simply because we can—we are making an investment that will pay not only big dividends in personal satisfaction but also in beneficial effect on others.

Recently, my teen-aged son asked why he had to study his lessons and make good grades. I explained to him that he had a keen mind and all of the ability he needed to score in the top ten percent of his class. So he should do well to please himself.

"If you were able to do only B or C work, I would settle for B's and C's. Since you can do A work, then you should bring home A's," I said. "Otherwise, you will be cheating yourself, settling for less than you are capable of producing. And you really wouldn't be happy with yourself."

Anyone who does his best naturally feels a sense of pride. Even a loser who has given his ultmost enjoys the comforting satisfaction that he did not fail because of negligence or indifference.

Despite the logic of living and working in this manner, many young men and women question the justification for hard work, dedicated effort or the superior performance.

"Why work when it isn't necessary?" That's a common argument. You also hear, "Why should I try to be superior? Who cares?"

If for no other reason, we should want to be superior because it's the natural desire of man to succeed, rather than to fail; to be admired for his competency, rather than censured for shortcomings.

Perhaps the best argument for doing a creditable job is simply that it prevents your feeling guilty. The person who does his best—and knows it—gains a sense of accomplishment, inner pride and self-confidence that money cannot buy. Besides, considerable evidence exists to prove a close relationship between awareness and conscience. If we don't want to suffer, we must put our best effort into each undertaking. Anytime we knowingly settle for less than the best we demean ourselves and must pay the penalty in loss of self-esteem.

Whether we admit it or not, a man is still his own severest critic. Millions of emotionally-ill persons in this country speak tragically of the harsh manner in which we judge and punish ourselves. To succeed is not merely a source of pleasure; it is apparently a necessity for healthful, happy living.

There seems to be no satisfactory substitute for winning, simply because you know in your heart you can win and wish to prove it. Merely to assume that you could succeed if necessary—without actually taking action to verify it—is a waste of time. It might even leave in one's mind the suspicion that he would have failed if he had tried.

Spinoza observed that, "So long as a man imagines that he cannot do this or that, so long is he determined not to do it—and consequently, so long is it impossible to him that he should do it."

Thoreau felt that man's capacities had never been properly tested or measured, and Pubilius Syrus suggested that "No one knows what he can do till he tries."

As we advance in life, we must inevitably accept certain limits on our abilities, but it would be a shame to apply those limits too severely or too soon. *No one knows what he can do until he tries!*

One Step at a Time

One morning a pretty housewife served breakfast to her family, saw her three children off to school, watched her husband leave for work, and then sat down to write a note:

"Don't try to find me. I'm going away."

Three days later when the frantic husband located his wife, she was resting safely in a motel room a few miles from home.

"I had to get away," she explained tearfully. "Things all seemed to close in on me. I just couldn't handle everything!"

Life *does* have a way of piling up on us at times. Almost every day we find ourselves with a long list of duties to perform, some simple and some serious. If a housewife made a count of everything she had to do from the moment she got up until she went to bed, the number might well total more than a hundred for a single day.

Even though many of the daily duties we perform can be completed in a few moments, the sheer weight of a multitude of chores, deadlines and responsibilities can bear down like a ton of troubles on a person's mind.

Unless you take measures to cope with a situation like this, you may go to pieces, or like the Red Queen in *Alice In Wonderland,* you may simply run madly just to stand still. In either case, life can become a madhouse.

A well-known radio announcer was complaining to me about the trials and tribulations of his profession. "Sometimes it gets so hectic in the morning," he said, "that I almost explode. All at once it seems I'm trying to keep up with news and music, time signals and weather reports, plus communicating with a couple of radio cars and a helicopter, and delivering a bunch of commercial announcements. It all looms up in front of me at times like a monstrous mountain and momentarily I get petrified."

In all walks of life similar situations exist. Business men frequently flounder in despair at the end of the day, mired in an avalanche of uncompleted jobs. Students often become distraught at the prospect of trying to complete all of their school assignments before bedtime. Sometimes an older person will find the matter of wrestling with two or more appointments on the following day a cause for great nervous concern.

Clergyman Harold Blake Walker has commented on the stress of everyday living and suggested that there are three aspects of the irrelevant which disorder our minds. The first is tomorrow crowding into today, looming ominously overhead. The second is today with all of its problems pushing and shoving their way into our mind, each demanding immediate attention. And third, "yesterday intrudes itself into today and the past haunts the present."

So our tension and anxiety stems from multiple sources, and the situation seems to grow a bit more difficult to cope with each day.

Perhaps the entire matter of living with stress and strain can be accomplished by adopting one simple motto: *Take one step at a time.* You can do a great deal to overcome your nervousness and bring your disordered mind into some state of calm if you will teach yourself to ignore what lies ahead, forget what is past, and concentrate solely on the task facing you at this moment. What has happened and what is to be are of no consequence if we are solely occupied with here and now. The mountain to climb is not the distant peak but the one looming straight ahead; and it can be scaled by stepping carefully, moving up one foot at a time, from one ledge or jutting rock to the next. Each toehold is a problem and deserves complete attention. Only after your foot is firmly placed are you ready to make the next step upward.

But what about the immediate problem? Which one should you tackle if you have an appointment book loaded with twenty different matters and meetings that must be dealt with during the day? The answer lies in putting priorities on projects, and this is just as vital to the housewife or school child as it is for the businessman.

Take a few moments at the beginning of the day to get organized. Decide the descending order of importance of the jobs you have to do. By allowing reasonable flexibility for accommodating the unexpected caller or the emergency meeting, you will find that most daily tasks can be assigned a proper place and time on your work schedule.

Putting first things first immediately relieves your mind of worry about whether you are neglecting something or not. The happy result of this orderly thinking and systematic procedure is that you can make each decision and take every action in an atmosphere of relative calm. You are able to concentrate fully and creatively on the specific matter at hand. Then one-by-one you continue through the day, like a doctor with a well-timed succession of appointments, until you have worked your way through a formidable, but no-longer-frightening, series of detailed discussions, phone calls, and letters read and answered.

With planning, patience and the right approach, a mountain of work can be reduced to a molehill of reasonable duties. The secret is simply to take *one step at a time.*

Flattery Will Get You Somewhere

Despite the busy lives that most of us lead, it is encouraging to know just how many thoughtful people take time each day to say nice things to others. Often the compliments are made to a friend or relative, but many times their words of commendation go to complete strangers.

Hardly a day goes by that I do not receive one or two brief, complimentary notes by mail. It is rare that I recognize the signatures of the writers; but in most cases they have heard me say something on a radio broadcast with which they profoundly agreed, and they have taken time to pen a few words of appreciation.

Anyone who is considerate enough to do this deserves the utmost praise, for there is no finer gift that you can present to another person than to say something nice about him. No diamond baubles or solid gold ornaments can equal the right words said at the right time to make someone feel loved and appreciated. Such phrases as "I love you," "I need you," "I am proud of you," are priceless in their power to create happiness.

If you want to make a lady in your life smile with joy and go through the day feeling marvelous, perform the kind and simple act of bestowing a compliment. Tell her you like the dress she is wearing, or better yet, how well she looks wearing it. Admire her hairdo or her radiant smile. Keep in mind that a positive compliment is much more valuable than one that recognizes a change for the better. For example, telling a woman that she appears to have lost weight and looks much better suggests that she did not look well when she was heavier. In such cases, the intended commendation may not be appreciated at all. But if you praise someone for being extremely attractive and alluringly slim, without intimating that this is a change for the better, the flattering words will find more receptive ears.

Flattery works just as well on men as it does on women, and it is equally effective on youngsters and grownups. We are all walking through life wanting to be noticed, admired and applauded. If a person repeatedly fails to get this satisfaction, he may become embittered and seek in reckless ways to fill the emptiness in his life. He may wind up being notorious instead of famous; feared and hated instead of respected—condemned instead of applauded.

Consider how much better it would be if everyone understood the universal need for recognition and the therapeutic value of flattery. We all respond to admiration. Even the most hardened cynic who frowns and snarls that you don't mean the nice things you are saying about him, secretly hopes and believes that you do mean them.

I have been impressed time and again to find how quickly a few generous, well-chosen words can melt an individual's heart and make him not only agreeable but extremely grateful. Edward Young speaks in *Love of Fame* about

> The love of praise, howe'er conceal'd by art,
> Reigns more or less, and glows in ev'ry heart.

A friend of mine has a trick mirror in the den of his home. It has a push button at the bottom of the frame. When someone stands before the glass and pushes the button, a message appears, superimposed over the reflection, reading: "You look wonderful."

"I've watched dozens of women go through the ritual of pushing that button," said my friend, "and never yet have I seen one fail to smile and look deeply pleased."

Apparently even the impersonal compliment, the kind you get from Chinese cookies, has a value! As Wordsworth knew only too well, "We live by Admiration, Hope and Love," and our lives are spent in longing for all three, regardless of whether we find them or not.

Being thoughtful and kind in your remarks to someone is a simple but sure way to make yourself liked. One of the most beloved men I know spends several hours each Sunday afternoon driving around calling on sick and shut-in friends. To each one he brings a present. It may be flowers, a book, or a box of candy. I once suggested that this was both a time-consuming and expensive way to spend his time. He replied that the gifts he bought cost far less than some of his acquaintances spent each Sunday afternoon for a round of golf. "And I collect a bonus," he said. "The golfer only benefits personally from going out to play, but I make a lot of people happy

113

while I'm satisfying myself. It's the greatest feeling in the world seeing the appreciation in someone's eyes when he realizes you think enough of him to come calling, bearing a gift."

Of course, tangible offerings aren't necessary to endear yourself to another individual. Your presence, or your voice, or even a written communication from you is all that is needed. "I can live for two months on a good compliment," remarked Mark Twain.

It would be difficult to find anyone who believes otherwise. Even the diffident, timid and lethargic get a boost from being complimented. A flattering remark made at the right time can supply the strongest kind of encouragement and incentive.

One effective way to flatter others is to check the newspapers for announcements of people who have won awards, honors and advancements. Choose several names each day, then as often as you have time, drop a line of congratulations to each one. Several of my business acquaintances do this regularly as a means of establishing contacts with possible new commercial clients. One of my friends, an insurance salesman, writes a letter of welcome to every family that moves into the community. Not surprisingly, he sells millions of dollars' worth of insurance every year.

One of the dearest persons I know is a woman who retired several years ago after a long career of school teaching. She still maintains contact with many of her former students (who number in the thousands) by writing them letters and making phone calls whenever she learns of any good fortune that has come their way. She obviously believes, as did Sir Thomas Browne, English author and physician, that "Praise is a debt we owe to the virtues of others. . . ."

Like casting bread upon the waters, attention lavished upon those who deserve it comes back in many gratifying ways. As these lines from Gilbert and Sullivan's *H.M.S. Pinafore* remind us:

> You're exceedingly polite
> And I think it only right
> To return the compliment.

Nevertheless, some persons are leery of passing out or accepting compliments, because they feel that flattery is essentially artificial. Doubtlessly, many contrived compliments are uttered daily; but this is no justification for equating flattery with fakery. It need not be at all! You can say nice things about an individual without being extravagant or untruthful in your praise. Flattery can and should be honest, sincere and simple.

Once when faced with the responsibility of introducing as an after-dinner speaker a United States senator whose political views were quite apart from my own, I tried to write down favorable things that could be said about him. To my surprise, the list was quite long. Consultation with several newsmen supplied additional information. As a result, I was able to prepare and deliver an introduction that did not bother my conscience but still pleased the senator very much. Unquestionably, you can flatter almost anybody and do it with frankness and sincerity if you are willing to look for his good qualities.

There's much to say in favor of adopting flattery as an everyday habit, since it can be helpful on so many different occasions. Oscar Wilde has a character in *An Ideal Husband* remark that, "An acquaintance that begins with a compliment is sure to develop into a real friendship." He was probably overly optimistic, but few would quarrel with the proverb: "True praise takes root and spreads." A thoughtful compliment can work wonders in cementing relationships, healing wounded feelings, and getting much needed cooperation.

Some years ago I knew a bold, young man who even used flattery as an adventurous hobby to add spice to his life and to the lives of others. More than once I have watched him walk up to an attractive woman on the street or in an airport waiting room and, although she was a complete stranger, say something like: "Pardon me, Lady, but I couldn't resist telling you that you are absolutely beautiful." Needless to say, he would choose lovely looking women to compliment so he was being honest. Having had his brief say, the young man would then walk away leaving a befuddled, bewildered, but thoroughly delighted woman gazing at his retreating figure. "Never once have I been slapped or turned over to a policeman," he said when I once asked if he were not behaving recklessly. "I only compliment those whom I believe deserve it. Could anybody take offense at that?"

Rarely does anyone get offended at a justified and well-intentioned compliment. To be congratulated by friends or strangers when you feel that you deserve such applause is one of life's supreme pleasures, and the most hardened cynic is vulnerable to such words of praise.

Yes, indeed, flattery will definitely get you somewhere! It will help get you precisely where you want to go in this world.

You Can Overcome Handicaps

Frail and aged, the wonderful lady, Helen Keller, departed a world which she could not remember ever seeing or hearing. Yet she filled the lives of millions with beauty and inspiring thoughts. Struggling against blindness, deafness, and muteness, she triumphed to become well-educated, successful and renowned. Her life story has been told in books, on the stage, in the movies, and on television. After spending an evening in her company, Clifton Fadiman declared, "Compared with Helen Keller, most of us in the room seemed somehow handicapped."

Anyone who despairs of ever getting anywhere in life should recall what this little woman did. She proved that a human being can work a miracle and overcome virtually any obstacles or hardships.

Helen Keller once wrapped up her attitude toward life in these words: "I thank God for my handicaps for through them I have found myself, my work, and my God." Her mission became one of helping the afflicted and the helpless all over the world. For more than eighty years she believed and proved that "Life is an exciting business and most exciting when lived for others." She had a joyous certainty that her physical handicaps were not an essential part of her being, since they were not in any way a part of her mind. This faith was firmly planted in her student days when she first learned of Descartes' maxim: "I think; therefore I am."

As Miss Keller explained it, those five words waked something in her that remained throughout the remainder of her life. She found

116

at last that her mind could be a positive instrument of happiness, bridging over the dark, silent void with concepts of a light-flooded awareness. Indeed it was possible, as she demonstrated with remarkable skill and sensitivity, to create light and sound and order within herself, regardless of how chaotic the outer world might be.

What Helen Keller learned and proved, all of us can try to emulate. Few of us will be tested as severely as was she, so our chances for mastering our difficulties—and achieving whatever we wish—are really very good. We need only make the effort to prove it.

It has been wisely said that anyone who wishes to avoid troubles in this world must not be born in it; yet, difficulties need not always be a cause for unhappiness. A moment of adversity can be turned into an opportunity if it is considered a challenge rather than an overwhelming obstacle.

There is considerable evidence that difficulties even create in us a capacity to match our troubles. If we fail, it may be that we don't know how to call on our inner resources of strength, ingenuity and will power.

Captain Max Cleland served as a young army officer in Vietnam. One day when a truckload of ammunition was being unloaded, a live grenade fell to the ground, endangering the lives of many soldiers. Standing nearby at the time, Cleland fell on the grenade just as it exploded. He protected his comrades but was grievously wounded, losing both legs and part of an arm. Still, he refused to be discouraged or despondent. "I will simply readjust my life," he said. "I intend to live as actively and happily as possible."

What is a handicap anyway except an extra weight to carry, a burden to make us try a little harder? Historians believe that the attack of polio which left him crippled for life was the motivating force that transformed Franklin Roosevelt from an ordinary man into an extraordinary world leader.

If you are handicapped in any way, take heart. You may have to work a bit harder and exhibit an extra measure of courage and tenacity, but your encumbrance could prove to be the best friend you have. In overcoming your handicap, you may realize just how strong and capable you really are.

And Then Some

I once heard a famous business executive divulge the secret of his success. He summed up his illustrious career in just three words: "And then some."

As he explained it, he was a young man when he began to notice a very profound difference between what you might call average people and those who forged ahead to become better educated, more prominent, wealthier and more influential. Certain leaders jumped out in front and stayed there, pointing the way, because they did what was expected of them—*and then some*.

"I watched how these top persons operated," he said. "They were thoughtful of others, they were considerate, punctual, dependable— *and then some*. I noticed how they met their obligations and responsibilities fairly and squarely—*and then some*."

They could be counted on in an emergency—*and then some*.

So this man, who had learned the secret of success, decided to apply it to his own life; and it worked. He did become wealthy and he climbed to the top spot in his company.

Now he was standing before a group of younger business and professional leaders explaining the dramatically simple answer—the way to reap rich rewards by merely doing a job well—*and then some*.

I know an automobile service station that is unsually busy. The two men who own it are well off. They have prospered and they employ a large, competent staff of attendants. It is not difficult to see why they have done well. The moment you drive in to their station, two or three courteous young men swarm on your car, checking under the hood, wiping all the windows, requesting that they be allowed to vacuum-clean the inside of the car, checking the air pressure of your tires, including the spare tire in the trunk—all while your tank is being filled with gasoline.

I have talked with the owners of this service station on numerous occasions about their methods. They say it costs more to provide this kind of attention, but it pays off. They try to do what is expected—*and then some.*

And it works. It will work for you, too, whatever you undertake to do today, or any time in the future. When you're putting forth that big effort to be helpful, thoughtful, or efficient, do the job—*and then some.* And be prepared to collect the dividends that will surely come to you.

Ethics

Calling All Thieves

Everyone is a thief! Does it shock you to be accused, or do you doubt that it's true?

I had never given the matter too much thought—reasoning, I suppose, that the world has always had more than its share of law-breakers, but that most of us, including myself, were honest. Then I heard a professor of ethics say that everybody does a certain amount of stealing. This didn't mean, he explained, that just anybody would blithely put on a face mask and go out to hold up a bank. Few of us are so predatory or malicious. It's degrading, you may think, to be considered members of the same notorious fraternity as burglars, pickpockets and shoplifters.

The evidence, however, indicates that we behave in similar ways. True, the professional crook makes a living by preying on others. Amateurs commit illegal and unethical acts for other reasons, pretending all the while that their indiscretions are trivial because they generally involve small amounts and minor incidents.

The reckless youngster who wouldn't hijack an automobile will swipe its hubcaps and laugh it off as a big joke. And some who wouldn't dare steal hubcaps will pocket silverware and ashtrays from restaurants, justifying their actions as harmless souvenir-collecting.

One major airline lost so many knives and forks that it produced advertisements teasing the public for its pilfering habits. A security guard at Mount Vernon told me that tourists, who supposedly come to pay homage to the Father of Our Country, will pick up anything that is not carefully watched or nailed down! "They would walk away with every plank and board if we didn't keep a sharp eye out," he said grimly. This seems a strange way to show respect for the memory of George Washington, doesn't it? I am sure that the offenders do not consider themselves guilty of serious wrongdoing; but I have a theory that every form of illegality—even simple misbehavior for that matter —is a form of thievery. Crimes and misdemeanors are all variations on the same theme: taking something that doesn't belong to you. It may be as cruel and tragic as snuffing out a life, or it may be as minor as helping yourself to a couple of towels when you check out of a hotel room.

Even mistreatment of one person by another involves thievery of a sort. There are those who steal by taking advantage of another's peacefulness, patience or ignorance. Down through history the strong have taken from the weak, manipulators have taken from the careless, and opportunists have taken from the distressed.

There are some among us who feel impelled to tear down and not rebuild; and that is thievery, too. You can't get something for nothing, goes the adage, but gamblers keep trying, win or lose; and if they succeed, aren't they stealing?

During the depression of the thirties, my father extended credit to hundreds of destitute families in the county where we lived. Later when they were able, many of these people ignored their obligation to repay their debts. That's also a form of stealing. Dramatic proof of it came when a letter arrived one day, unsigned, and containing a ten-dollar bill. The sender wrote, "I have owed this to you for many years. I want to pay it before I die to clear my conscience."

It isn't the amount involved, or the gravity of the offense in the eyes of the law, that determines the seriousness of stealing. The real answer lies within each person's mind and heart. The commission of the act guarantees self-punishment, but unfortunately, we don't always restrain ourselves because the temptation of the moment is too great.

Anyone who bends his conscience to live by a double standard, reasoning that private property should be protected but the taking of public property is permissible, brands himself as one of the most hypocritical of thieves. He is a close comrade to the fellow at the office who filches ballpoint pens, stationery and rubber bands because they are too insignificant to matter. Actually, the purloiner of paper clips is just as dishonest, in his way, as the hardened criminal who blows open a safe and makes off with a fortune. Both are using the same phony logic to justify what they do.

A neighborhood grocery man once told me that he loses an enormous amount of fruits, nuts and candy to customers who help themselves to samples. Department stores, specialty shops and five-and-dimes are plagued by scores of adolescent shoplifters, many of whom come from well-to-do families. When caught, the youngsters usually explain that they steal merchandise just for the thrill or to qualify for membership in juvenile clubs that admit only proven thieves.

Parents are often astounded when they learn that their children have been arrested for stealing. How could it be? And yet these mothers and fathers have practiced dishonesty and deceit constantly in front of their youngsters. The slightly doctored information that Dad puts on an income tax form, or even the golf score that Mama or he falsifies, are attempts to gain benefits not justly earned. Sons and daughters who observe such behavior learn many lessons about dishonesty that were never intended to be taught.

Lest we think that all stealing is concerned with material things, it's well to remember that we also can and do steal intangibles.

One petty type of larceny is to impose on someone's time or talent, asking for assistance without any real intention of making a repayment. It's grand larceny of sorts to steal someone's heart, reputation or irreplaceable-self-confidence without attempting at least to make restitution.

The worst thievery of all is to steal from yourself. Everyone does this by wasting time, throwing away opportunities, dissipating health and creative energy, allowing friendships to wither and die. If you doubt that a human being can defraud himself, ask any sick, lonely, embittered person who has frittered away his life and regrets the cruel deceit he has played on himself.

Yes, we steal in many ways from ourselves and others; and we offer countless excuses for our actions. It may be that the commandment, "Thou Shalt Not Steal," is more demanding than even the devout can obey. Perhaps we can derive some comfort from realizing that we feel good inside not by achieving perfection, but by striving for it. The more sincere and trustworthy we are with ourselves, the closer we will come to living honestly and happily with others.

The Greatest Charity

When I was six years old, I belonged to the "Lucky Four Club." Each Saturday morning we would meet to play, eat refreshments, and to bring nickels which went into our charity fund. Eventually we collected three dollars and mailed it to an orphans' home in New Orleans. It was my first experience with charity and I liked it. There's no greater feeling in the world than the glow of satisfaction you can get from helping someone who really needs assistance.

Charity has even been termed by some Biblical scholars as the equal of all the other commandments. Throughout man's long history, he has been encouraged to consider the poor and the helpless, but it is well to note that you don't necessarily do this by handing someone money. In fact, a needy person may appreciate affection, consideration and benevolence much more than dollars. We all know kindly persons of limited means, who are very charitable. They do their giving in good deeds rather than dollars.

Being charitable is something that can be interpreted in a variety of ways. The simplest and least noteworthy manner of giving is to offer a dole to an outstretched hand. This will buy a hungry man a meal, but it won't help his self-respect. The open act of giving money to someone in need isn't a pretty picture. The fact that the donor and the recipient come face-to-face is a questionable practice. It smacks not of generosity but of ostentation.

While all charitable contributions may qualify as beneficial and commendable, the obvious gesture of making a donation does seem to suggest that the benefactor wants most to be recognized. It makes his assistance suspect. It indicates that the most important reason for giving is to be noticed and applauded, even if it embarrasses the recipients of his charity.

Moses Maimonides suggested back in the twelfth century that there are eight rungs of charity. The highest step involves helping someone to help himself.

This means that the noblest act of charity is something quite different from giving a handout; rather each of us is admonished to be much wiser and more compassionate. It tells us that charity is best when it is an act of sharing rather than an act of giving.

In some American cities, self-help programs are now in operation, for the handicapped, the poor and the culturally deprived. The approach is to provide education and training, encouragement and whatever economic assistance appears necessary. The purpose is not to give to the needy, but to help human beings emancipate themselves.

When this approach is made to work, it produces wonderful results. In time, a seemingly-hopeless derelict may become self-supporting and not need charity at all. He can stand independent and proud, the peer of his fellow Americans.

John Ruskin emphasized, "A little thought and a little kindness are often worth more than a great deal of money." He was trying to tell mankind that charity is not meaningful unless it comes from the heart, and is properly offered. The highest charity requires no press-agentry because it is not given with the intention of gaining recognition or receiving thanks.

This is charity above the public or private donation. It is charity of a type superior to an anonymous gift of a million dollars. It is the highest stage of charity—helping someone help himself to realize his full capabilities.

The Good Person

When a youngster seeks approval and affection he says, "I'm being good, Mommie."

This way of thinking never changes, regardless of how old we become. It's still comforting at any age to feel that we're "being good." Of all the words in the dictionary, "good" has the most wholesome, healthy, happy ring to it. We refer often to the "good person" and praise "good deeds." A woman need not be beautiful to be admired, but she must be good.

Goodness is a quality that we associate in partnership with Godliness, generosity, and a warm, forgiving heart. A good man is an honest person. A good woman is helpful, considerate and full of loving kindness.

There is a smile packed away in everything that is good, whether it be good news, goodwill or good cheer.

"Goodness is easier to recognize than to define," said W. H. Auden; but this did not deter the Biblical prophets, and it has not thwarted civilization's greatest scribes.

Aristotle asked what makes men good and conceded that nature might be responsible in some cases, whereas training and instruction deserved credit in others. The important thing is that the world is fortunate to have certain people who put goodness above greatness.

"Goodness is the only investment that never fails," said Thoreau; and John Wesley's *Rule* made clear his unswerving belief in the magnificence and essential values of goodness.

> Do all the good you can,
> By all the means you can,
> In all the ways you can,
> In all the places you can,
> At all the times you can,
> To all the people you can,
> As long as ever you can.

When men and women debate about how they should live and where their loyalties should be placed, it is significant that they agree on the desirability of being good. True, vast differences may arise about whether certain actions are legal, decent or desirable; but the opposing parties will both contend that they not only stand for what is right, but also for what is good.

What are some qualities of goodness on which there is universal agreement? A good person gives food to the hungry instead of indifference. He provides treatment for the sick and not neglect. He provides for the poor to be helpful, not to be praised. He offers personal assistance rather than impersonal donations. He loves humanity and respects individuals for who they are, not for the color of their skin or the religion they practice or the wealth they possess. A good human being believes in open doors, open neighborhoods, open minds and open hearts. He has only one standard, speaks one opinion publicly and privately, and believes devoutly in the oneness of humanity.

It isn't easy being that good, but it's fun to try!

> Good, the more
> Communicated, more abundant grows.
> Milton, *Paradise Lost*

There is joy and pleasure to be found in living a good life and doing good deeds. It is a source of lasting satisfaction for which there is no substitute. Generations after men and women are gone from the earth, think how the ones who are most kindly remembered are thought of in terms of goodness. Euripides saw this happening in his time.

> When good men die, their goodness does not perish,
> But lives though they are gone. As for the bad,
> All that was theirs dies, and is buried with them.

Can you think of any finer memorial to a person who has lived a full, productive and benevolent life than to say: "He was good"?

"His Word Was His Bond"

We attended the funeral of a good man the other day. He was an honest farmer who had lived a long, clean and honorable life. His wants had always been simple and his needs modest. He loved his children and took pride in their accomplishments.

During his more than three-score years and ten, this gentleman saw the world change from a rural economy to an industrial one. He saw mules give way to tractors, and trucks overtake wagons. He saw the kerosene lamp go out and the electric light turn night into day. He saw simple countryside turn into busy, bustling suburbs. As he watched, people moved faster, talked louder, lived more dangerously, acted more recklessly, behaved more ridiculously.

But this man stayed on the farm. He was a son of the soil. He continued to worship in a small church. He found solace under a shade tree, on the banks of a blue lake, chatting with his neighbors, sharing his worldly goods unselfishly with others, proving by his daily deeds that he knew no strangers and had no enemies.

This man did not get rattled by the changing times. And he refused to compromise his principles, despite any hardships or temptations that came his way.

One of the ministers who extolled his virtues said, "His word was his bond." You don't hear that term used much nowadays. Not many folks put stock in it like they used to, but it was important to this hardy American. And it is critically necessary that we find a way to make it important to a new generation of Americans today. Honesty, integrity, character are not passé. They are as necessary as they ever have been. The answer to many of our present-day problems lies in making these principles live again in the way we live and act and behave toward one another.

If we want an honest, efficient government, we must vote intelligently and support the conscientious efforts of honest and capable men.

If we want better communities, we must build them in cooperation with our neighbors.

If we want peace in our country, we must feel peace in our hearts; and we must seek understanding, not with guns or threats, but with goodwill.

This is not a time for letting someone else carry our part of the citizenship load. We cannot elect as president a magician who will wipe away our troubles, blast away our vexations, or bury our responsibilities.

Like the fine man whose life was full of honesty, integrity, and goodwill because he made it so, we must give of ourselves. If we want a clean, brave, renewed nation, each of us will have to contribute toward its building—and we must come bearing our gifts with faith, fairness, fidelity, and brotherly love.

Ego and Conscience

After Napoleon's army took a terrible beating at Waterloo, and the emperor's majestic legions were strewn across miles of bloody battlefield, this vain and pompous little man still had the nerve to declare that he was going to rebuild his armies, hold firmly to the allegiance and loyalty of all Frenchmen, and proceed to conquer Europe.

Did he really believe what he was saying? In the face of a galling and overwhelming defeat, how could he persist in the myth of his invincibility?

A century and more later, the story repeated itself with Adolph Hitler. He was obsessed with a madman's vision of power and greatness, and he held to the dream of conquering all his foes virtually up to the minute that he took his own life in a Berlin bunker.

Did he honestly believe this? I suppose he did, in the way that a

129

sick, feverish mind may be haunted by visions and hallucinations that seem real even though they are not. Contrast these men of history with the humanitarian, Winston Churchill, another strong figure, but one dedicated to liberating, not enslaving, mankind.

For the truth is that the rational mind accepts certain limitations—but not limitations on dreams or hopes; no not even limitations on ambitions, provided these aspirations do not intrude on the rights and privileges of others. There is the dividing line. The man of good mind and goodwill knows that he must serve two masters: his ego and his conscience.

The two must be balanced. The need for self-fulfillment must not be allowed to trounce upon the need for respect of others. When this does happen, a man becomes a tyrant. When the two are in balance, a man becomes a great and good leader.

Do What Is Right

What's happened to good old-fashioned respectability? It seems to have been tossed in the trash can of discarded virtues.

The popular phrase now is: "Do your own thing . . . don't worry what anybody else thinks." An emancipated younger generation speaks of free thought, free speech, free love and freedom to spit in the face of respectability.

"There was no respect for youth when I was young," lamented J. B. Priestley, "and now I am old, there is no respect for age—I missed it coming and going."

Perhaps many parents did not show enough respect for sons and daughters of generations past. Now the tables are definitely turned, with many young people exulting in the opportunity of being openly disrespectful of their elder's mores and morals.

I can understand defiance of traditions that have outworn their usefulness, and I can condone a person's unwillingness to show respect for something which he does not respect. But I doubt seriously anyone who says that he does not want personally to be respected. Even when a snarling young rebel smears his face with paint, dresses in rags and lets his hair grow like sagebrush, I think he is pleading to be noticed; and in his own pathetic way, he is begging to be respected.

I do not believe Bertrand Russell was serious when he said, "I have always thought respectable people scoundrels, and I look anxiously at my face every morning for signs of my becoming a scoundrel."

The declaration may raise eyebrows but it doesn't ring true. It isn't natural to want to be a scoundrel, but it is natural to crave respectability. Famous men hope to be remembered by historians as decent beings with noble ideals. Granted, many fall short of the mark; and it's not uncommon to see respectability treated shabbily by some who pretend to be better than they are. But the fact remains, however, that a man's real life is decided in great measure by the respect others have for him. Take away a person's self-respect and you destroy him; build up his self-esteem and you open up a new life for him.

How do we merit more confidence and esteem from others? Socrates offered a simple answer: "The way to gain a good reputation is to endeavor to be what you desire to be." When you give convincing evidence that you hold yourself in high regard, you induce others also to consider you deserving of special recognition.

This doesn't mean that you should pose as something you aren't. It does suggest that you demonstrate the qualities you wish to have noticed and appreciated. If you are honest, reliable, compassionate, others will notice and respond favorably. Not every respectable person is handsome or wealthy; but if he is honest and good, there is a clean wholesomeness about his character that money can't buy. It will show itself in the way he acts and talks and does business. His real worth will make itself evident to others whether he wishes such recognition or not.

Life has been compared to a pair of sensitive scales, weighing each of us constantly to determine our real worth. What we accomplish, or fail to do, shows itself quite clearly in our appearance and behavior. A happy person demonstrates his feelings by the way he faces the responsibilities and surprises of each new day. A cheerful disposition beams like a neon sign, telling everyone that you relish duties, affection, and even what Helen Keller called, ". . . the bright crystals of delight hidden in somber circumstances and irksome tasks."

Have you ever noticed, though, how many faces are etched with lines of dissatisfaction and bitterness because recognition has passed them by? It's regrettable that so many want to be respected but unknowingly, or unwillingly, fail to earn what they cherish most.

You've seen the tense, anxious individual who walks around with a chip on his shoulder as though he's convinced that others are going to misunderstand and mistreat him. Actually the abnormally-sensitive person mistreats himself—and blames others. He looks everywhere for the culprit except in the mirror.

The world is shaking today from millions of incomplete persons who shout their contempt for whatever is respectable and sneer at the traditional measurements used to gauge the worth of a human being; but their words aren't convincing. They profess not to want admission into the fraternity of compliant and cooperative humanity, but their bitter tirades are a sham and a masquerade. Each longs desperately to be accepted and respected.

"The mother of all lies is the lie we persist in telling ourselves about ourselves," said Thomas Merton. This is repeatedly proved by those who are crying inwardly for love and respect but hide their loneliness by their cold and suspicious manner.

Eleanor Roosevelt was a sensitive woman who might have allowed herself to become an embittered recluse because of her plain appearance, a domineering mother-in-law with whom she lived for many years, and an eminently successful husband. Instead, she maintained her composure and self-confidence, becoming in time one of the world's most respected and honored citizens. "No one can make you feel inferior without your consent," she advised those who sought her advice.

Abraham Lincoln also believed strongly in the redeeming quality of self-respect. "It is difficult to make a man miserable while he feels he is worthy of himself and claims kindred to the great God who made him."

Mark Twain said, "Always do right. This will gratify some people

132

and astonish the rest." It will do more, for in the long run this is the way to build and maintain a solid reputation for integrity and dependability. Do the right thing, tell it like it is, and respect yourself as much as you want to be respected. This is the responsible way to become a memorable person, admired by many, loved by some, and respected by everyone.

Feb '87

Human Relations

Keep Collecting Friends

You can never do much about selecting your relatives, but you can name and cultivate your close companions. It is your fault if you fail at this most important undertaking: the winning and keeping of true friends.

Your happiness and your effectiveness depend in great measure on the relationships you establish and maintain. It might be possible to go through life as a loner, without developing any warm and comforting relationships, but it would be a pretty bare and cold existence. There are times when we urgently need someone to talk with, an understanding person to go to for advice. That's why friendship can be invaluable.

My wife and I once tried to decide to whom we would turn if a critical emergency demanded immediate help. The person we thought of was a friend that we rarely see but have a special fondness for, and we know that he feels deeply about every member of our family. In time of need, he would be our choice.

135

Do you have such a friend? They are rare but they are wonderful. If you don't feel such a closeness with someone, you should. Certainly a friend can fill a place in your life that no one else is able to do. Santayana thought, "One's friends are that part of the human race with which one can be human." Suffice it to say, we are talking about a very special type of person. He can sometimes advise you about personal and business matters better than members of your immediate family. He can also be closely concerned with your problems, and yet exercise a valuable objectivity in giving you an opinion.

A friend often sees through to the heart of a matter when we may be so close to it that our emotions threaten to overrule our reason.

Even the most devoted married couples find that they need friends in whom to confide. An extremely thoughtful husband does not always lend the most attentive ear to his wife. A devoted wife may be unable to comprehend all of the technical problems that a husband wants to discuss. That's when special friends can step in to fill a unique role.

How well should you know someone before you call him a trusted friend and share with him some of your innermost thoughts? That question arises frequently as we meet neighbors or club members and wonder just how close to be with them. Each friendship should develop as a distinct relationship and be judged on its own merits. Generally you can decide after a few weeks whether someone should remain a casual acquaintance or move up into the privileged category of being considered a confidential pal.

Living as most of us do today, it is probable that we will often meet persons whom we initially like, but conditions will not permit us to make them into fast friends. Homes are far apart and day-to-day meetings may be impractical. So the lightly-involved friendship can be expected to play an ever-increasing role of importance in our lives. You should take care, however, that you do not misjudge it for something of greater significance. You could easily be disappointed. Remember, if you have played only a brief, minor role in someone's life, he can hardly be expected to have developed a deep affection or concern about your troubles.

If you want a friendship to be of special importance, you must work to make it just that. Fortunately, a whole world of humanity is waiting to get better acquainted, so you need never be without as many good friends as you are willing to develop. What this boils down to is, showing a sincere and continuing interest in someone else's life. The more you find out about an individual, the easier it is to talk with him, to appreciate his good qualities and forgive his bad ones. Eventually you are able to relax in one another's company without feeling the need to be especially nice or talkative.

In fact, Clifton Fadiman has suggested that one measure of friendship is its ability to exist without a lot of conversation. In other words, the better you know someone, the less you need to bother with amenities. In fact, most of us would prefer that a friend level with us when necessary. "Don't spare my feelings, tell me what you think," is the kind of statement you want to be able to say to a friend and confidante.

Often we seek out and hold onto comrades who share opinions similar to our own. They don't always make the best friends because their thinking is too predictable. You should try to have at least one friend who is able to disagree with you without being disagreeable. Everyone needs to know and feel affection for someone capable of expressing a fresh viewpoint, offering a criticism in a spirit of good-will.

So, in many ways, a good friend should be an extension of yourself, supplementing your own talents to make you more efficient and effective than you would be alone. In fact, a good friend will even substitute for you, pleading your case when you cannot do it, handling your tasks when you are ill or incapacitated. Best of all, he will listen when you need to talk and talk when you need to listen.

You can always tell your best friend by his ability to reassure you at your moments of doubt and deep despair. When you are embarrassed, he convinces you that you should not be. When you've made a fool of yourself, he proves to you that you haven't done a permanent job.

During dark moments when you feel that the rest of the world has walked out on you, in walks your friend, picking up the broken pieces of your hopes and dreams, volunteering to run interference for you in your pursuit of happiness.

There have always been some cynics who have belittled friendships. Afraid to trust his feelings in another person's keeping,

Voltaire prayed, "May God defend me from my friends; I can defend myself from my enemies."

But most of us realize that living would be a drab, lonely and uninspiring existence if there were no friends to share our good and bad moments. "The beauty of enmity is insecurity; the beauty of friendship is in security," wrote the poet, Robert Frost. There is a warmth, a glowing sense of well-being that comes from having a trusted friend.

As we become older, and our long-time comrades start to disappear from the scene with ever-increasing frequency, we should be making and retaining new friends to take their place. When he heard of the death of Dwight Eisenhower, Field Marshal Montgomery, frail and eighty-one years of age, lamented, "All my good friends are leaving me."

Fortunately, anyone with a lively interest in the present, and an open mind toward the future, need not be left without companions. If you have a genuine desire to like and be liked by others, you can make friends at any age. Studies of hundreds of elderly men and women have been made and it was found that they had amazing ability to develop new acquaintances that often ripened into warm friendships. Perhaps we make friends easier as we grow older because we are not as competitive, suspicious or greedy as in our younger years. In time we learn to appreciate friends not for what they own, or can do for us, but simply because they make possible a comforting union of kindred minds and spirits.

"Collecting friends is my hobby," a smiling retired minister once told me. It's a great way to spend your time. Cultivate friends intensively before you need them, never taking for granted the consideration you receive, and never stinting on the affection you give. "Behold, I do not give lectures or a little charity," wrote Walt Whitman, "when I give, I give myself." And Mark Twain believed that the joys of life, to be fully appreciated and understood, must be divided with somebody.

That's the starting point from which friendships can grow and blossom. You need only give the project some heartfelt attention. Above wealth and fame, you will find with the passing years that the dearest of all possessions are friends.

"The Times They Are A-Changing"

"What is happening?" That question comes to mind often as we wrestle with the most topsy-turvy, perplexing problems and crises any generation has ever known. We are assailed not only here at home but all over the world by what has been appropriately called "tough choices and hard decisions." Newscasts on radio and television and the music of the younger generation tell us, "The Times They Are A-Changing," a fact we know only too well as we are bounced back and forth between our dreams and our dilemmas.

We love peace but we find ourselves at war.

We are an affluent society but it's a fact that our poor, our ignorant and our hungry number into the millions. We sing the praises of *America the Beautiful,* but we are steeped in all manner of ugliness. Our air is polluted, our streets congested, our rivers are contaminated, and our slums are growing like weeds.

We pay lip service to truth and honor; but some of our people aren't sure what truth is and, therefore, daily dishonor themselves, their fellow men, their institutions, and their American citizenship.

We all agree that courage and heroism are fine qualities; yet many of us do not recognize genuine heroism when it is demonstrated before our eyes, and we are just as likely to condemn the man of real courage as an outrageous show-off.

We praise patience as a virtue but we rarely demonstrate forebearance in our dealings with others.

We relish the comforts and conveniences that have resulted from our dynamic, changing economy; but many of us turn around and denounce change itself as an evil.

We send our children to college to broaden their knowledge and their viewpoint, only to find some of them squatting defiantly in the classrooms to deliberately stop the academic process.

More and more of our people realize the need to live in and earn their paychecks from our magnetic cities, but we incessantly curse the troubles and confusion that result from crowded metropolitan living.

We pay homage to the great leaders of history and revere the prophets of antiquity who tried to point the way to the good life; yet we constantly harangue the contemporary prophet who dares say that we must give of ourselves to others if our own existence on earth is to have any meaning.

Now that is a pretty sobering list of problems, isn't it? We have come to a point in history where it's impossible to go fishing and get away from the cares of the world. If we stand still, we are asking to be run over; so what can we do to bring a measure of composure and sanity to our lives? The answer lies in getting involved, becoming a solver of human problems, and admitting that we are, indeed, our brother's keeper.

"We cannot afford the luxury of escapism," a prominent industrialist told me. "Every American must answer the call of his conscience and of his neighbor in need." This means seeing the world as it really is and recognizing every other person in it as someone worthy of love and understanding.

After working for several months as a volunteer teacher of children in a poverty neighborhood, a mother confessed, "I perhaps should be embarrassed to admit this, but these children have taught me for the first time how precious other human beings can be and how cruelly they have been penalized."

It is a revealing and touching experience to become involved in helping someone. Caring for one person can sometimes teach us to care for all humanity. The human mind best understands people problems when it thinks in terms of a single person. Human difficulties, even though they may be of massive proportions, are really individual problems that must be dealt with one by one.

Unfortunately, the crisis of our times has not registered on enough minds. Too many are still unaware, unconcerned and uncommitted. They do not think of being helpful, because they have not come face-to-face with fellow humans in need of sympathy and help.

And sad to say, a great many of those who deserve the most assistance are the hardest to reach. Some are hidden in slums and rural hovels. Others make themselves known, but only to express their bitterness and disillusionment, and to resist the overtures of "outsiders" whom they resent and mistrust.

It is easy enough to ignore need when we do not see a suffering person or hear his cries for help. It is doubly easy when the individual in need says he doesn't want help. The key question that must be asked is: is your offer made with your own outstretched hands? Many of us are willing to be charitable if we can do it at a distance. Our attitude reminds me of the *Saturday Review* cartoon showing a couple dressed in evening clothes passing a cripple with hat in hand. The cripple is saying, "Know the joy of helping someone without the slightest danger to yourself of getting involved." We must get involved and become personally aware of the human beings we are duty-bound to help; for no one wants to be the recipient of charity, but everyone longs to be loved, respected and recognized. Always there is the inner self crying for recognition and gratification.

Herein lies both our greatest challenge and our biggest hope. I am reminded of Edwin Markham's lines:

> He drew a circle that shut me out—
> Heretic, rebel, a thing to flout.
> But Love and I had the wit to win:
> We drew a circle that took him in!

Every time an idle youngster is rescued from a poverty neighborhood he is nourished with the precious qualities of self-esteem and pride. Each time a business concern takes on its payroll a disadvantaged employee, it is investing not merely money, but faith in another person's spirit and potential. And every such individual's success becomes a walking, breathing testimonial to the American free-enterprise system.

The fearfully prejudiced think only in terms of being invaded by a mass of unwanted humanity. That humanity, however, consists of individuals who deserve and demand freedom to choose where they shall live, the jobs they shall qualify to fill, and the lives they wish to enjoy. The matter of open-housing brings the whole urban situation into sharper focus than anything else, because it calls on each American to comply in a manner which will prove his devotion to the democratic ideal.

When Lincoln Steffens was fighting hard against the shameful conditions of our cities, he said that he was appalled by the silence of the good people. I am equally appalled at their stubborn selfishness. Millions of so-called good people are completely indifferent to the sufferings of the less-fortunate, and appear unwilling to make any concessions for creating a more just and equitable society.

Once when I delivered a broadcast editorial outlining what we must do to achieve true equality, an irate listener phoned to complain. When I asked if I had said anything incorrect or unjustified, the caller answered, "No, what you said was right, I guess, but I'm just not ready to do it."

Consider, if you will, the price that will be paid if we do not get ready, if we fail to meet our moral obligations. Even if mothers and fathers and children were willing to be contained within restricted borders, their very numbers could only produce mounting ills and pressures, leading eventually to violent explosions. Realistically, we know that the ghetto must go. It cannot be preserved legally, and it cannot be justified by any humane standards.

Mark Twain once remarked that a crime persevered in a thousand centuries ceases to be a crime and becomes a virtue. We must not continue trying to find virtues in a criminal caste system based on skin pigmentation. Our Declaration of Independence speaks of full freedom, liberty and justice, not for the group, but for the person. And so does our Constitution.

The editor of the *Saturday Review,* Norman Cousins, has declared: "The ideology of democracy begins with the idea that man owns himself—owns his mind and body and the right to his full growth as an individual. He is the most important unit in his society. Nothing that his government owns is as precious as he is. No government should have the right to tell an individual what to think or believe or what he should do with his life."

Regrettably, most of our thinking about social problems has been based on the cruel assumption that one individual can tell another what to think and believe, where to live, and how far he can go in this world. This is an unwarranted infringement on another human's rights and has been outlawed, but it still exists in a thousand hidden forms of bondage and discrimination.

Is it any wonder then why some individuals react so violently against this state of affairs? We may condemn their actions as irresponsible and dangerous, but we must not blind ourselves to the conditions that promote rebellion. Unhappy, frustrated persons either hide away or fight. Many become drug addicts, commit crimes, lash out wildly at a society which they feel enslaves rather than liberates. If we want to change the course of their lives, we must offer each one more than token citizenship, token rights, or token responsibilities.

Individual freedom is a precious possession, but it cannot be half-given or half-lived. Freedom and accountability are twins, permanently joined, and must be experienced completely if democracy is to have any meaning or value.

Some of our people are too comfortable and indifferent. Others are too angry and revengeful. One wants to maintain conditions as they are, and the other wants to destroy what he considers worthless. Both are tragically wrong. They do not realize that a government which proposes to be free can only function through the consent and participation of all the governed, and an open society must be free to everyone if it is to be safe and secure for anyone.

George Washington declared that a nation of people can enjoy only as much free government as they are individually willing to obey. Each of us must strive to live and work with one another in such a manner that we really are sharing the privileges and the burdens of American citizenship.

Where the free citizen is handicapped, we must allow him to overcome his deficiencies and develop his potentialities lest we all suffer from his shortcomings and his inability to carry a fair share of the load.

Above all, we must not let the desperation of a minority or the inflexibility of a majority conspire to prevent reconciliation or to block reform.

Oftentimes we hear the phrase, "Education is the answer." This is only partially true. We do need education; but it must be accompanied by real opportunity for individual economic and social advancement, or it could prove to be more harmful than helpful.

You cannot give a person the benefit of increased knowledge and build up his ambitions without also giving him the chance to move ahead according to his talents.

Shakespeare said that the miserable have no other medicine than hope. When we give transfusions to keep human hopes alive, we sometimes achieve remarkable results. In some cities, entire factories already have been staffed by men and women straight out of the slums—and the experiments are working.

America cannot buy obedience from embittered rebels; but if this nation allows its citizens to move up as far as their abilities and ambitions warrant, it gains something infinitely more important—the loyalty and respect of the people.

James Russell Lowell put it so well:

> Be noble! and the nobleness that lies
> In other men, sleeping, but never dead,
> Will rise in majesty to meet thine own.

The Bigots Among Us

Crackpots call at midnight. Drunks call at two in the morning. Some bigots call any time. If you are a broadcaster who editorializes and voices strong opinions about human rights and responsibilities, you're bound to receive complaints from many quarters. You come to expect phone calls and letters and even to welcome the rational criticism offered by a responsible citizen who is willing to identify himself.

The sickening communications are another matter, especially the anonymous ones. They are the work of nasty, little minds hiding their identity but not their animosity. When the phone rings, it's always pretty much the same routine; "No, I don't want to give you my name, but I want to tell you what a lousy, stinking. . . ." After that comes a string of obscenities and foul accusations, wild, reckless, venomous. More often than not, the anonymous hate letter is poorly typed or scrawled out as though written by a hand trembling with

144

rage. It does no good to write a reply. Your letter will only return marked, "Address Unknown."

As you might imagine, there's a common streak of fear and ignorance running through these communications. Each protest discloses a little person with no pride, no courage, but a great deal of greed and suspicion. Lonely and insignificant, he feels a desperate need to condemn and downgrade others. It is his mixed-up method for making himself more important.

I used to get upset having to listen to a late-night caller's irrational diatribe, but now I feel only sorrow for anyone with such a spiteful, malevolent attitude.

Upon opening the abusive letter, I have learned to smile patiently at the outlandish charges and the misspelled words. The more of such scurrilous material I read, the better I am able to visualize the pitiful character of the writer. His is the futile cry of a frightened animal.

"The mind of the bigot is like the pupil of the eye," said Oliver Wendell Holmes. "The more light you pour upon it, the more it will contract." A fanatic will recoil from the light of reason. He is terrified of having pried loose from his grasp the preconceived notions that motivate his life.

In Alexander Pope's *Epistle to Dr. Arbuthnot,* fanatics are described in this manner:

> Fire in each eye, and papers in each hand,
> They rave, recite, and madden around the land.

They do untold damage in their rampaging, for bigotry has been called the child of ignorance and the father of prejudice and persecution.

I have never met a bigot who I believed was ignorantly sincere about the poison he was spreading. Deep down in the simplest mind is a realization that religious and racial hatred are something vile and loathsome. I have looked into the feverish eyes of a hate merchant and seen awareness of guilt; the haunted look of a man resigned to paying some day for his sins, but determined to drag down as many victims as possible before he slides to destruction.

Aldous Huxley has contended that "Most ignorance is vincible ignorance: we don't know because we don't want to know." Unwilling to listen to reason, the fanatic is driven by a mad desire to assert himself.

Incapable of dominating in any legal or ethical way, he resorts to the only method he knows—indecent attacks on decent human beings. This vicious sadism is tough to cope with because fair-minded men find it difficult to defend themselves against outrageous and reckless charges.

The most effective way to deal with prejudice peddlers is to expose them. Even though they may wrap themselves in the American flag and stand in pulpits pretending to be righteous, they are still vulnerable. These social misfits can best be dealt with by revealing publicly their lack of knowledge, the infantile approach they make to problem solving, and their obvious ruthlessness and brutality. When the bigot is questioned in an open forum, his true character shows itself in frightening detail.

Not so easy to identify unless you meet him face-to-face is the sly hypocrite. He doesn't write nasty letters or make obscene phone calls. He's the smoother type who waits until he is comfortably settled among those with whom he feels secure; then he quietly expresses his arrogant and prejudiced opinions. This is the individual who may pose as a benevolent and fair-minded citizen; but much of his goodness is manufactured by press agents, and anything he says about loving his fellow man is a mockery of the truth.

No man of small virtues can lay claim to a good character. If he does, he is either deceiving himself or trying to deceive others. His fakery may make him the worst of all the bigots; for while he pretends to have high principles, he is really a creature of the lowest sort, demonstrating his weakness and his ugliness by what he secretly says and does.

It is possible to test a person to determine if he is really generous-hearted and dedicated to fairness for all mankind. Find out if he is honest with himself. Find out if he loves truth. Find out if he has the courage of his convictions. And lastly, determine whether he is compassionate.

Anyone who possesses these qualities cannot hide them. They will mark him as a person who loves other people and proves it not by words, but by the way he lives.

146

One Man's Junk Pile Is Another Man's Treasure

Every month or so my family will load up the trunk of the car with trash and assorted junk (gathered from around the house) and drive with it to a nearby community dumping ground.

There a peculiar thing always happens. For each item we discard, we see something else lying on the junk pile, inviting us to pick it up and take it home. What a neighbor considers useless and expendable may very well interest someone else as being not only attractive but potentially very valuable!

I remember the day we drove to the trash heap to discard our trunkload of expendables. My son and I immediately spied a pair of bicycle training wheels lying nearby.

"Son, if we can find two more wheels to go with these," I said, "we can build a racer or a wagon." So we threw the wheels into the trunk of our car. Then we added a pair of iron pipes that I decided quickly would make a foundation for a muscadine arbor, plus a couple of pieces of lumber that I had no immediate use for but still recognized as worth saving. A moment later we picked up some sample bathroom tiles, an unusual length of chicken wire, and a battered but challenging footstool.

When we arrived home, the reaction of the wife-and-mother did not equal the positive enthusiasm of the father and son. But it did point out vividly the fact that what one person is ready to throw away, another is ready to accept with welcome arms.

This applies not only to inanimate objects, but even to human beings. The business world is full of elderly men and women, who were retired from their jobs, only to find excellent positions elsewhere. None ever gets too old to be productive. Consigning a healthy human being to the inactive list is not only unfair treatment, but it deprives society of another bright and useful talent.

One of the most fascinating persons I ever knew was an old New Englander who collected sea shells. When I first met him, he was in his eighties, operating a small shop on the Maine coast. During the tourist season he would display and sell some of his thousands of magnificent specimens. He told me that he had been a sailor, but after getting too old to go to sea, he had become a drifter. One day he was walking along the beach, feeling depressed, unwanted, when he noticed a shining shell, glinting in the sun. It beckoned to him with a message.

"I found a new life and I've been happy ever since," he said.

When the old man died a few years later, his will stipulated that his shells be given to a local museum. It was one of the finest collections to be found anywhere.

This illustrates the hidden talents that may go unrevealed—unless someone brings them out. Many persons are unable to overcome their handicaps, as this sailor did, but they might if given assistance.

Before passing by the useless-looking person, or pitching out what appears to be trash in your basement, consider carefully what you are doing. Are you dismissing as worthless, some person or possession that deserves to be cherished? Will someone else take the time to study possibilities that you do not see?

Sometimes we give up too quickly on friendships because they seem to have outlived their usefulness, when actually the relationship may simply be starving for lack of proper understanding and attention. When we fail to find another person interesting, it is possible that we aren't trying hard enough. Don't discard another human thoughtlessly. Your collection of friends, unlike inanimate objects, dwindles through natural attrition, and should be nurtured carefully through the years.

A number of the brightest minds in the world were unwanted orphans, who might have died on a trash heap somewhere unless they had been rescued by loving arms. Many of the greatest inventions waited for centuries to be discovered. Oil oozing out of the ground in Pennsylvania was a nuisance to homesteaders there until the internal combustion engine created a demand for petroleum.

So don't heedlessly toss anyone or anything on the junk pile. Take another look. Judge with your heart as well as your head. Make sure that you are right. Otherwise, you could be giving away the finest treasure you've ever owned.

Change

The Eleventh Commandment

If Moses had come down from the mountain with eleven commandments, I suspect the additional injunction would have read: "Thou shalt accept change."

Despite the reluctance of so many persons to adjust graciously to changes, there is evidence aplenty that this is the most certain of all things. "Life is change . . . How it differs from the rocks," sings a contemporary musical group. Each human being was created as a dynamic creature destined to develop mentally and physically, always to be a different person tomorrow from what he is today.

We were born to live courageously and daringly, human enough to fear the unknown but brave enough to relish exploring it—yet many of us fall far short of the mark. We shun change without bothering to ask, "Is it good or bad?" We grow nervous at the very thought of new ideas making our lives different. "The world is changing so fast," we say, "it must be going to the dogs."

Has mankind always been so timid and afraid? Run over the names of the great men and women you can recall. Were they shy souls who followed the crowd, conformed to the thinking of their associates? Were they horrified at the thought of change? Certainly not. The Bible speaks of Moses going against authority and tradition to preach for change. Jesus of Nazareth advocated change.

Socrates wanted change and progress, even though it cost him his life. So did Galileo, Dante, Darwin. And so did the rebellious souls who fomented and fought the War for American Independence. Indeed, they felt it was time for a change.

Within the last century, our nation has fortunately produced a number of courageous persons who were dissatisfied with well-enough and determined to make changes for the better. At the time Thomas Edison invented his first electric light bulb, millions of Americans wouldn't allow such an invention in their homes. Kerosene lamps or candles were good enough, they reasoned.

Many citizens thought the first automobile was not only a silly idea, but they considered it a dangerous nuisance as well, because it frightened their horses. As late as World War I, the top field marshal in Great Britain declared that automobiles would never replace horses as weapons of war. Think how silly many people must have considered the first breakfast cereal turned out by Dr. Kellogg, or the first rickety airplane of the Wright Brothers, or the theory of an atomic reaction advanced by Einstein.

These crazy, impractical ideas that have changed the face of the world and the course of civilization were the brain children of people who refused to conform because they realized that progress demanded sensible change.

Some years ago Rachel Carson dared to warn us that we were poisoning our fields and streams and the air we breathe. Her courage in speaking out drew abuse down on her head, but now her wisdom is being vindicated and noticed.

There are many other pioneers trying to break through the forest of fear and confusion, telling us not to resist new ideas, but to welcome them.

They keep asking us not to act like robots, not to be an army of think-alikes, but to get involved in what's happening—to behave as

150

individuals with God-given minds and voices that are uniquely our own.

But it is one thing to advocate freedom of thought and action, and quite another to make it a reality. Martin Luther King, Jr., exhorted man to change his feelings; so did Robert Kennedy. We adapt to technical changes much more readily than to social ones.

When a next-door neighbor displays colossal stupidity or ugly prejudice, most of us are reluctant to voice disapproval or to try changing his mind. We prefer to play it safe, gritting our teeth and keeping our mouths shut. But is this right? Are we not defaulting on our duty as human beings?

Our alarming disassociation from the world around us was evident when a woman in New York was stabbed to death by an assailant. Twenty-seven persons heard the woman's cry for help. Not a one stepped forward. They all explained: "I didn't want to get involved." Reports of millions of hungry children in this country leave most of us unmoved. Crime is a problem of all our people but few volunteer to do anything about it.

The late President John F. Kennedy emphasized that few generations have been granted a greater opportunity to serve our fellow man than have we. "I do not shrink from this responsibility—I welcome it," he said, urging the American people to join him, to take a stand on the picket lines of progress.

Don't we owe his memory the respect of at least checking our performance record?

In his book, *Change, Hope and the Bomb,* David E. Lilienthal tries to show that change, like growing older, is a natural process, one that we can turn to our advantage, if only we will. Yet, persons and groups continue to resist change and condemn it as evil!

A listener calls a radio station to complain because she resents news of student upheavals and civil rights disturbances. "Why do you report the bad news?" she asks. "Give us good news." As if the disturbing events would not occur if they were ignored!

An elderly man, who remembers when America was literally isolated fifty years ago from other continents, bemoans the fact that we are not still enjoying that same splendidly secure isolation. And he blames it all on a conspiracy of spies and Communists, who he says are trying to "change" things in order to bring about the downfall of this government.

Doubtlessly, some embittered revolutionists want to see this nation falter and fail; but that could happen only if we allowed it and, like a worn-out prize fighter, became tired, disillusioned and inflexible, incapable of adapting to the challenges confronting us.

Certainly we must not deny ourselves or our children access to the original and stimulating thoughts of mankind. Imaginative and oftentimes disturbing theories have sparked every dynamic action, every major change since the dawn of civilization.

Rigidity, opposition to change and progress grow from what we don't know and are reluctant to find out. We *must* overcome ignorance and fear. If we let the people know, they will respond. They must see and hear to understand. We can lessen tensions, increase understanding, and improve human relationships by communicating the realities of a changing world. We may not agree with every angry young writer whose paragraphs are full of despair and protest, but we must safeguard his right to speak. We must be farsighted and recognize that many of the things that people say and do, the ideas they create, and the causes they espouse, may not be bad but merely misunderstood. A symphonic work by Stravinsky, booed by those who first heard it, has lived on to be acclaimed a masterpiece by a succeeding generation.

If at first we do not comprehend fully what our fellow citizen is trying to say, let us listen and do our best to establish communication. Whatever is said should stand or fall, not on its ability to pass a censorship test, but on its public acceptance or rejection in the arena of free competition. If we do not like the reckless rumblings of our younger generation, let us not stop at rebuking the rebels but try to find out how much of their criticizing is valid and what can be done about it.

A long time ago, benevolent old Benjamin Franklin advised: "Without freedom of thought there can be no such thing as wisdom; and no such thing as public liberty without freedom of speech, which is the right of every man, as far as by it he does not hurt or control the right of another; and this is the only check it ought to suffer and the only bounds it ought to know."

Another wise, good man, Mahatma Gandhi, observed that freedom is not worth having if it does not connote freedom to err, to make an honest mistake.

Let us respect the "Eleventh Commandment" to accept change, and never try to stop the wheels of progress. Denouncing or prohibiting thoughts and opinions will only run them underground. We cannot silence the spokesman of new and alien ideas by forbidding him to speak; for he will be heard, even if he must use devious methods or resort to violence.

Let us, rather, be strong and secure enough to let the dissenter, the advocate of change, whether he be logical or illogical, mature or childish, have his say, confident that the voices of common sense and good judgment will still prevail.

Turning Points

There's a turning point in every person's life. Many of us experience a number of small turning points, and at times we are forced to work our way around big turning points as well. A big turning point is one that may determine the career you follow, the person you select to marry, or whether you enjoy a full, rewarding life or experience more than your share of bitterness and defeat.

Turning points are sometimes simple and quiet episodes that you encounter on uneventful days. More often they are dramatic—perhaps even agonizing—affairs that torment your mind and torture your soul.

The Scriptures are full of stories about people who reached turning points. Cain, Samson, Jonah, Job, David, Judas—all faced moments of crisis and decision. Some elected to go onward and upward; others chose to take a selfish or expedient course that resulted eventually in disillusionment and tragedy.

Sometimes, of course, turning points are reached unknowingly:

Lincoln's decision to attend Ford's theater, John F. Kennedy's determination that he must go to Dallas, Texas. These were unrecognized turning points. On the other hand, Harry Truman's decision to use the atomic bomb in World War II was a calculated turning point in the history of all mankind. President Lyndon Johnson's touching conversation with his daughter, resulting in his decision not to run for re-election, was a turning point of vital importance.

Most of us don't realize that we, too, are constantly reaching turning points, just as surely as famous and infamous persons of the past have done. The big question is: Are you making your turning points achievements of which you can be proud and from which you will derive satisfaction in years to come?

You may be debating at this moment whether to seek another job or join an organization. You may feel that you are on the verge of a turning point in your relationship with a family member or friend. Ponder your turning point well, not on the basis of what will please you at this moment, or of what will temporarily or conveniently solve a vexing problem. Remember that turning points must be lived with from now on, for they set you on a completely new course.

An incident in the life of Napoleon tells why many persons fail to manage turning points properly. On the eve of a great battle, Napoleon was discussing strategy with one of his generals. "But Sire," the general asked, "what will we do if the circumstances are against us?"

"Circumstances!" Napoleon answered, "I make circumstances."

Indeed, we make our own circumstances. We are responsible for most of our own lucky and unlucky breaks. In other words, we arrive—of our own doing—at turning points that decide our destiny.

We should make every effort to see that we control our turning points in sound and sensible ways.

Keep On Keeping On

The late Adlai Stevenson was fond of a story that he attributed to an aged man in his hometown of Bloomington, Illinois. When this ancient gentleman reached the marvelous age of 100, a reporter went out to interview him and asked the very natural and expected question, "How did you manage to live so long?"

The centenarian thought for a moment and began ticking off the items on his fingers, "I never smoke. I never drink liquor. I never overeat. And I always go to bed early and get up early. I've lived this way all my life."

The reporter looked puzzled and then said, "Well, sir, I had an uncle who did those very same things, and he only lived to be eighty. How do you account for the fact that he didn't live as long as you have?"

"He didn't keep it up long enough," came the reply.

There's a lesson in this anecdote, which is too often overlooked or underrated. Many of us start out with good intentions, but we grow tired or discouraged and abandon our best ideas before they have had time to produce results.

Name almost any invention and you can find earlier similar devices that were conceived and tested by others. Each was not pursued diligently or long enough to prove its worth. A sound idea is often neglected until someone later—with more foresight and perseverance—makes it pay off.

Every school child in America thinks of being president of the United States. Precious few make it. The late President Kennedy decided that he wanted to reach that exalted goal years before he was elected. He went to work, planning his strategy, devoting endless hours to a long-range campaign until he reached his goal.

We should check up at times on the chapters of our lives that are yet to be written. What incomplete stories do you intend to finish?

What projects have you neglected that can be important to your future success? The real test is your willingness to give what is required, to stay at each important task until you see it completed. If you want to prove that you have the energy and patience to make your life bigger than it now is, you need only keep on keeping on.

Awareness

Are Kids Really Confusing?

Why do grown-ups says that they are mystified by the thoughts and actions of youngsters? It hasn't been too many years since parents of adolescents were themselves in their teens. I doubt seriously that mothers and fathers have such unreliable memories that they cannot summon at least a few vivid recollections of their own youthful idiosyncrasies.

I know that it is easy to recall many of my thoughts and feelings as a high schooler and later as a college student. Hardly a day passes that I do not see and hear my son behaving in ways that remind me of myself at his age.

If my teen-age boy is careless about leaving his belongings scattered around the house, I may be annoyed, and I may recognize the need to correct him, but I also remember that I did the same thing when I was a boy.

On a more serious note, when my son wants to talk about the

stupidity of war, the hypocrisy of many who profess to be most pious, or the failure of our society to correct what everyone admits must be corrected, I hear echoes of my own complaints years ago.

Many youngsters are different from teen-agers of twenty-five or thirty years ago in their willingness to voice their concerns and, when sufficiently aroused, to openly demonstrate their emotions. It is this teen-age tendency to be frank and open and uninhibited that creates most of today's grownup consternation.

With most youngsters, I suspect that they are merely talking openly about what their parents talked about secretly, and perhaps doing unashamedly what many of their elders did but never admitted.

It seems to me that the most serious problems we have today with our youngsters are not a result of revolutionary new ways of thinking. Kids think pretty much as they always have. They have a natural inclination to be inquisitive, idealistic and experimental.

Unfortunately, millions of boys and girls find that their parents are afraid to be inquisitive or experimental—and most disillusioning to youngsters is to learn that so many of their elders do not think it is safe or sane to be idealistic.

Adult cynicism is at the root of much of our youthful rebellion. It has caused many mothers and fathers to neglect giving their children the guidance and supervision they need; and, most importantly, it has robbed youngsters—at their most impressionable age—of the right to believe in both the possible and the impossible dream.

Keep Your Cool

"Keep your cool" has become an accepted phrase in the American language, and it makes a lot of sense. Getting steamed up over the annoyances of everyday living is easy to do, and it's understandable; but you'll be much better off if you remain calm and refuse to fly off the handle.

Losing your temper over every little disappointment may not only rob you of valuable time and energy, but indignant outbursts can also be hard on your digestion and play havoc with your peace of mind. Millions of sick, sad people are victimized by their own tempers. They take life's setbacks so seriously that every thwarted expectation becomes for them an invitation to a battlefield encounter.

Remember the phlegmatic character in *For Whom the Bell Tolls,* who repeatedly met abuse and adversity with one simple rejoinder? Whenever challenged, he invariably replied, "I do not provoke."

That's a sound way to face your tormentors and tempters: keep your cool and refuse to be provoked. You'll win more than a victory over your foes; you'll also achieve an important triumph over your own fears and doubts. The easy thing to do when hard luck or frustration is hounding you is to get angry, to throw in the towel and admit by your exasperation that you're incapable of coping with your own temper tantrums.

Those who succumb to their feelings and strike back blindly every time things aren't going right inevitably shrivel somewhat inside. However, if you can remain calm and unruffled during heated moments, especially when others around you are rattled, you'll not only acquit yourself properly, but you'll be happier as well.

Dr. Walter Alvarez, the famous consultant, has warned of the consequences of taking our troubles too seriously. Don't walk around with a chip on your shoulder, he advises, daring everyone to disagree with you because the chances are you'll find plenty of takers. Quick-tempered people have a penchant for getting involved in situations that compound their dissatisfaction. They usually wind up doing a pretty thorough job of driving off friends and making themselves embittered and lonely.

Despite all this evidence in favor of the cautious and reserved approach, the emphasis in recent years has been on speaking out. The meek are told to give free expression to their feelings of hostility and aggression. "Don't be inhibited" has become a dictum for the distressed and the timid. "Let yourself go!"

Now the time has come, I think, for re-evaluation of this recipe for mental health through emotional release. Letting yourself go and flying off the handle may not achieve a beneficial result at all.

Aristotle understood the volatile and unpredictable nature of anger when he wrote: "Anybody can become angry—that is easy; but to be angry with the right person, and to the right degree, and at the right time, and for the right purpose, and in the right way—that is not within everybody's power and is not easy." As a result, "Anger, if not restrained, is often more hurtful," according to Seneca, "than the injury that caused it."

Doubtlessly, the angry person damages his own self-confidence when he loses his temper, but he also frequently hurts others in the process. In many cities, and on numerous college campuses, riotous anarchists have swung their mallets against authority, tradition, rules and reason, but their unreasonableness has offended and frightened even those who originally sympathized with their cause.

Unbridled anger also may be responsible in great measure for the chaotic situation existing in so many homes. In our efforts to disprove the adage that silence is golden, we have promoted free speech of dubious value.

For fear of repressing and warping youthful personalities, we have created a whole generation of angry, irresponsible rebels, many of whom talk much more than they think. Some of these young militants have no compunctions about yelling "Fire," in a crowded theater, or perhaps even setting fire to the theater if they dislike the patrons or the feature attraction.

Dr. Bruno Bettelhein, psychologist-professor of the University of Chicago, has suggested that the wreckers and burners of this age are demonstrating by their uncontrolled rampages that they are "very, very sick" and in need of psychiatric care.

They may also be proving that while it is not right to be a slave to anger, neither should anyone become a tyrant because of it. Speak when you're angry and you'll make the best speech you'll ever regret. This is the point that needs restating strongly, along with the advice that when you lose your temper, you generally lose a lot more as well, ending up sadder if not wiser.

"Anger and folly walk cheek by jowl," said Ben Franklin. "Repentance treads on both their heels."

Anger has been defined as an uncontrolled feeling that betrays what you are when you are not yourself. Any time the irresistible urge to explode starts welling up within you, cool it, and be glad that your better self is winning a victory for composure, maturity and common sense.

You Look Great

Are you satisfied with the way you look? If so, you're a rare person and doubtlessly a wise and mature one.

Just about everybody I know dislikes his appearance and would change it if he could. We are a people obsessed with fear of being unattractive. We spend millions on cosmetics, clothing, surgery, and psychiatry, to make ourselves appear more as we want to be.

Hardly anyone is exempt from the desire to look less like himself and more like someone else. I heard television star, Johnny Carson, confess one night that he would enjoy being two inches taller, although he is a successful six-footer and is enormously popular. On the same program, actress Phyllis Kirk said that she would completely remake her face and figure if it were possible, despite the fact that she is considered a very attractive woman and is widely admired and imitated.

For fourteen years Jimmy Durante played the piano in vaudeville without once speaking to the audience. He was afraid that people would laugh at him for being homely. Little did he know that millions of admirers all over the world would come to consider his warm, smiling face as one of those they most enjoyed seeing.

Why are so many men, women and youngsters displeased with the way they look? One plastic surgeon and long-time student of the subject, says that most of us have a poor opinion of ourselves; our self-image is badly in need of repair.

Despite the Biblical admonition to "Judge not according to the appearance," most of us insist on placing an abnormal importance on appearance, especially our own. We too rarely believe that "Handsome is that handsome does" because of our obsession with real or imagined defects in our appearance.

Convinced that he was too ugly to ask for the love of Roxanne, Cyrano pleaded the cause of another suitor, only to find belatedly that his long nose did not in any way affect Roxanne's love for him.

Many times our friends admire us for physical features that we consider repulsive. The Roman profile that offends so many who possess it, has been a source of immense pride to a long succession of emperors, actors and business tycoons.

Walt Whitman wrote:

> Of the terrible doubt of appearances,
> Of the uncertainty after all, that we may be deluded.

Nowhere is greater doubt or uncertainty exhibited than by the self-conscious person who dislikes and downgrades the face that stares back when he looks in the mirror.

One method that I've heard recommended for building self-confidence and improving a self-image is simply not to look in the mirror. Out of sight, out of mind, is the theory. Besides, the mirror sometimes lies. It throws back more than one reflection of the person gazing into it. The image that you see is only what your own eyes perceive, and your own mind judges! You appear differently to others because they see you as a composite of many qualities.

This suggests then that your displeasure with yourself comes not from what you see in the looking glass but rather from inner visions that can only be erased or altered by changes in your thoughts and in your opinion of yourself.

Socrates prayed that he might be "beautiful within." Anyone who possesses this feeling has little vanity about the short-lived tyranny of outer appearances.

Perhaps the best way to combat those unhappy feelings of inferiority that plague us about our looks is simply to concentrate on living a full and good life, realizing that others see us for what we are and not merely as one-dimensional physical beings.

When we create a shining character for ourselves, it tends to make our imperfections diminish, or even disappear, and our sterling qualities emerge. We become more and more attractive to others.

162

A good woman, admired and loved by her family and friends, is almost invariably thought of as a lovely and handsome person. Have you ever known a devoted mother to be anything but beautiful in the eyes of her children? Gorgeous heroines exist almost exclusively in the pages of fiction. Memorable women become so, not by being good-looking, but for more substantive reasons.

When a man is elected president of the United States, the public has enormous interest in what he says and does, but little critical concern with how he looks. If millions have voted him into office, this indicates approval of his general appearance.

When there is some comment about his ears, mouth or chin, it is usually spoken in good-humored jest, for the truth is that the exalted post of Chief Executive makes any occupant of the office look attractive and inspiring to most of the people.

The same is true of kings and queens, movie stars, and celebrities in all walks of life. The better they are known, and the more widely they are admired, the better they seem to look. Abraham Lincoln has often been referred to as a homely man. More than one historian has described him as awkward, ungainly, even ugly. Yet, millions look at his photographs, or gaze at the imposing statue seated in the Lincoln Memorial, and marvel at the kindness, compassion and gentle strength of his wonderful face.

This should convince us that it is not only unhealthy but unnecessary to dwell on such trivialities as the color of one's eyes, the plumpness of a figure, or the size of the feet. Relatively few people know or care that George Washington had red hair beneath the powdered wig that he wore when posing for portraits, or that he had false teeth. We remember the Father of the Republic for what he said and did.

In similar fashion, the people who know you and love you aren't concerned with precisely how much you weigh or the exact shape of your face. They feel close to you because you have won their respect and affection. Consequently, they like you as you are, and the way you look.

The contented person accepts the fact that he could not drastically alter his outward appearance without changing his inner-self as well, and for many this is both unnecessary and undesirable.

Most of the celebrated comedians have developed their insight and humor not by hiding their deficiencies, but by relating their own faults and defects to the weaknesses they see in others. It is doubtful that any humorist could be genuinely funny or convincing if he were a flawless physical specimen. Bob Hope and Danny Thomas have profited from the way their noses fit on their faces. Jack Benny laughs with the millions who love his effeminate walk, as well as his miserly reputation. Flip Wilson gets laughs by referring to the color of his skin and his experiences with racial bigots.

Beautiful and ugly are only relative terms at best, and they differ considerably from one generation to another. The words also have different meanings in various parts of the world. Life will be happier and more enjoyable for all of us if we learn to accept differences in human beings as a natural phenomenon. Dissimilarity should in no way be misconstrued to imply superiority or inferiority. Most of the distinctions, and all of the discrimination that develop from differences, are man-made. Nature is not so prejudiced.

If you will be fair to yourself, and moderately grateful to your parents and the Lord above, you will have to admit that most of us were not short-changed in looks or intelligence. With few exceptions, you were given features that may be different, but are the equal of any person on earth. You need only accept your physical and mental inheritance with pride, and realize that your feet, regardless of the size shoe you wear, will take you just about anywhere your mind has the desire and determination to go.

Be Proud

How proud are you, my friend?
You should be intensely proud for you are a mortal marvel.
Think what you can do with your God-given talents.
With your hands you can reach out in friendship to strangers, and with your fingers write a letter to someone lonely.

With your arms you can lift the weak and the fallen, play a game with a child, or embrace a loved one.

With your eyes you can see a world of infinite promise, and glimpse a multitude of incomplete projects begging to be finished.

With your ears you can hear the sweet call of opportunity and answer its challenging appeal.

With your lips you can utter your thoughts, freely and fully, and kiss your beloved with unrestrained devotion.

With your mind you can dream and plan, outlining the route you wish to follow toward a happier future.

With your legs you can walk in the direction you choose, selecting the destination your talents and ambition direct.

With your senses keenly alert you can touch and feel, smell and taste, see and hear all that's fascinating, mysterious and exciting in this universe.

How marvelous your versatility!

How infinite your powers to question, to perceive and to master your destiny!

You are indeed a wonderful person, blessed a thousandfold with strength and wisdom, patience and perseverance, imagination and idealism.

What will you do with your greatness?

Will you share your abilities and blessings with those who are less fortunate?

What contributions will you make to help your fellow man?

What legacy of charity and noble deeds will you leave to the world?

How much of your magnificent potential will you multiply through others?

How proud are you of the gifts you possess?

Are you selfless enough to submerge your pride in acts of kindness and compassion?

Are you generous enough to share your mind, your heart, your faith?

Are you gentle enough to love all men?

Are you proud enough to be humble?

How proud are you?

Take Your Time

What's your hurry? When you see a man rushing to catch a plane, or a driver stepping on the gas to beat a traffic light before it turns red, aren't you tempted to ask that question?

"Rushitis" is a great American disease, but it isn't a new illness. The Koran declares, "Haste is of the devil," and an old Russian proverb says, "Hurry is only good for catching flies." Obviously, for centuries victims by millions have been obsessed with scrambling, scampering and plunging headlong into every new experience. The afflicted rush to work and rush to play. Everything is on double-quick time. Golfers scoot around the course on electric carts, too nervous to relax, too tense to walk from hole to hole at a leisurely pace. Mothers clean house and prepare meals as quickly as possible, intent only on getting through. Youngsters wear out games and toys in a matter of moments as though struggling to beat a deadline, and then become restless and irritable, anxious to skip off in search of new diversions.

We're all familiar with the motorist who isn't satisfied to drive within the speed limit. He has a compulsion to exceed it, frantic to save five minutes in getting somewhere, even though he does nothing important after he arrives.

Never have so many people scrambled, scampered, and dashed madly through life as if the next moment were to be their last on earth. The compulsive speedster jumps out of bed each morning ready to tackle a back-breaking schedule of jobs that he is convinced must be done immediately. He bolts down a scanty breakfast, rushes to the office, and immediately gets mired up in so many different worrisome projects that the day usually ends in confusion and unfinished business.

Anyone who insists on hastily finishing more tasks than he can properly handle may as well expect to wind up doing none of them well. In the process, he will probably get awfully tired and needlessly unhappy.

Shakespeare advised, "Wisely and slow; they stumble that run fast."

Try as you might, you can only complete one job at a time, and to do that properly you must first acquaint yourself with precisely what you are attempting to do and the best way of tackling the task.

Despite the logic of this approach, it's amazing how many Americans still insist on doing everything the hectic, hard way. Housewives will hurriedly open a bottle of cleaning fluid and start applying it to a dirty garment without taking ten seconds to read the directions for proper usage.

Some years ago a pilot, "Wrong-Way" Corrigan, took off in an airplane, apparently headed for California. Instead, he flew across the Atlantic Ocean to Europe. Asked about the wrong direction, he explained that he had misread his maps. Whether he actually did or not, the episode reminded millions of Americans that they, too, were often guilty of rushing off in the wrong direction.

A moment or two taken in deciding what to do, and how to do it, need not be time wasted. And once you embark on a project, you shouldn't feel that you are loafing on the job if you stop occasionally to rest or to evaluate what you are doing. Even in automobile racing, where there is tremendous emphasis on speed, the drivers are constantly checking themselves and their competitors, taking stock of how many miles they've traveled, how far they have yet to go, and the best strategy to use in finishing victoriously.

Molière claimed that "unreasonable haste is the direct road to error." To illustrate how too much hurrying, and not enough thought, can penalize the violator, I have seen dozens of men and women fail a simple speed-and-aptitude test. The test contains a list of 25 operations that are to be carried out. The first instruction at the top of the page says clearly, "Read everything before doing anything and then work as quickly as possible." Then the next 24 assignments consist of problems to be solved, plus a variety of serious and foolish procedures to be followed. Since it is a speed test, most people hurry to complete everything on the page, only to find out when their paper is graded that they have flunked. They have neglected to follow the initial instruction, which requires that the test-taker read everything before doing anything. If this first requirement is met, it leads eventually and naturally to the final line on the page which says simply: "Now that you have finished reading carefully, do only sentence 1 and sign your name at the top of the page, say nothing, sit back and watch the fun."

Ben Franklin was right. Haste makes waste. Those who rush to finish a task they do not understand are flirting with trouble. They misread, make numerous mistakes, and do not enjoy what they are doing because they are concentrating on getting through rather than completing a satisfying assignment.

Years ago John Ruskin noted, even though he lived in an age of horse-drawn carriages, that the faster we travel, the less we enjoy the journey.

We shouldn't misread any of these observations as an endorsement for slowness, but it does suggest that we miss a lot when we get into too much of a hurry.

I have a friend who travels by train, even though it frequently takes him a day or more to get from one city to another. "I don't think about the hours being wasted, because they aren't. I have time to work, to think, to see the country, and to fully appreciate the meaning of going from one section of the nation to another." When you cross the continent in a few hours, you frequently become disoriented. On very long trips it is not unusual for a traveler to become ill because his human time clock has become upset by rapidly passing through so many time zones.

Of course, we have to allow for the fact that we live in an age when speed is important, and rapidity is often not a matter of choice but of necessity; but we can minimize the pressures on our daily lives by eliminating as many speed-up operations as possible. You can start by making a daily list of things you need to do. Try to undertake first those jobs that are crying for immediate attention. Do only one assignment at a time, handling each carefully, efficiently, through to completion. At the end of the day, you may find that you've finished everything on your list. If not, look over what you have left and see if it can wait until tomorrow or perhaps even be struck from your schedule.

From time to time you will want to make additions to your daily work sheet. As you add an item, put it in its proper place on your priority list.

Following these few simple steps should take a lot of rush-rush out of your life and replace it with a great deal more calmness and peace of mind.

Real Happiness

The Search for Real Happiness

"Happinesss" has become a very fashionable word in the American vocabulary. Songs, cartoons, books, movies all use it. And more and more advertisers are tempting people to buy products for the joy, pleasure and happiness that ownership will bring into their lives.

One observer has suggested with more seriousness than jest that the time is not too distant when supermarkets and department stores will feature happiness departments. There you will find all of the articles designed to brighten your mood and bring on an inner glow of contentment and satisfaction—everything from antidepressant pills to solid gold toothpicks.

Why are we so engrossed with this mad search for the happy life? What compels us to gratify every selfish whim or desire, even to the extent of going enormously into debt, or at times drastically changing the whole course of our lives in a bid for happiness?

Apparently, being hipped on happiness is a reflection of both our prosperity and our disillusionment. Millions of our people are no longer worried about food, clothing and shelter. Jobs are abundant, and money is available. Basic needs have been satisfied. In many ways we've never had it so good. But just as these are the best of times, so are they the worst of times as well. Many men and women have fat bank accounts but are morally, ethically and spiritually bankrupt. So they understandably seek ways to fill the emptiness of their lonely, unrewarding lives.

This frantic search manifests itself in many ways. Some rebellious youngsters dress in outlandish costumes, smoke marijuana, take drugs, sing protest songs, make speeches, and march. A desire for bigger, flashier automobiles, fancier clothing, memberships in clubs, travel to foreign countries, ostentatious houses, acquisition of fine books, rare paintings and vintage wines—all of these are obvious symbols of affluency and are not in themselves objectionable. Unfortunately, many who wallow in luxuries are sick, sad, anxious and grievously self-centered. They keep trying to buy a happiness cure-all despite overwhelming evidence that anxiety cannot be cured with self-indulgence; and the elusive butterfly of happiness cannot be caught in a gold-plated net.

Other civilizations have known such times. Both the Greeks and the Romans had their troubles with too much money and too few responsible citizens. The sobering results of their follies should be a lesson for this age, but more than a hundred fallen civilizations prove that mankind doesn't learn as much as he should from the mistakes of his predecessors.

Today the cardinal principles of love, justice and truth have too little influence on our behavior. Most of us are motivated by the lure of greater material comfort, security, prestige, and a degree of mental isolation which we conveniently label "peace of mind."

What has brought on this wave of existentialism, this crying need for self-gratification? Part of the answer must lie in our evolution to the computer age, where millions of persons have been reduced to numbers on credit cards, and many resent mightily the loss of their individuality. Already machines are doing so much work that human beings are having to find new avenues to expend their energy and release their creative impulses.

We have reached a state of technical development where man is both a scientific wizard and a social infant, frightened by the bombs he has built and frustrated by his seeming inability to defuse them. Man has been described as exploring outer space, living in a spiritual kindergarten and playing in a moral wilderness.

The times, then, are not of man's choosing; but he is caught up in the turmoil and, in many ways, contributes to the maelstrom he so desperately wants to avoid.

Can we find real happiness in this chaotic world? Surely we must to survive; and certainly we will because man still is, as always, a creature driven as much by faith, hope and dreams, as by desires.

"Man is the only creature that refuses to be what he is," said Albert Camus. The great objective of this generation must be to find meaning in our drastically changed social and scientific order. As long as human beings inhabit this earth, there will be need for mutual trust and consideration. Instead of simply catering to our self-seeking interests, we can and should use our prosperity, our leisure time, our vastly expanded knowledge to help others, and to work with them in beneficial ways.

We are born to be dynamic and restless and adaptable. We need only continue to prove it. The future will require that we liberate ourselves from the frozen attitudes and fixed expectations of the past.

Now as never before we must understand that happiness cannot be bought or bargained for, but only developed inwardly as a by-product of loving relationships and worthwhile activity. So we must temper our affluence with charity and compassion, truth and maturity.

Certainly we have staggering problems to contend with; and we have reasons aplenty to be frightened, dejected, enraged. It is also a fact that we live on the edge of a precipice, but the mature person understands that we are on the brink of that cliff together. Philosopher Martin Buber explained this well when he said, "Life is not lived by my playing the enigmatic game on a board by myself . . . Original guilt consists in remaining with one's self."

Real happiness will be found by the human being who willingly and gladly offers consideration and love to someone else, exchanging the monologue for a dialogue, the closed fists for open arms, the selfish mind for a kind and generous heart.

The Most Important Day
in Your Life

One day on a radio program I heard a number of persons commenting on the most important day of their lives.

Some women said it was the day they got married. Others said it was the day their babies were born.

One man said it was the day he decided to quit his sinful life and start on a new pathway.

A youngster smiled and said the most important day of his life was the day he was born. "Otherwise," he said, "I wouldn't be here."

But the answer that I remember most vividly was the one of a man who said: "The most important day in my life is today."

He went on to explain: "Yesterday is gone and can't be relived. Its mistakes are history. Better to leave them buried in the past. Tomorrow is in the future and may not be at all as I might imagine. So the really important day in my life is right now—to live as well and as completely as I can."

That made good sense to me. It still does. And I'd like to share a few thoughts with you about this most important day in your life. A day of new beginning. A day of unlimited opportunity. A day for working miracles and transforming your life.

It was Shakespeare who noted that

> Come what come may,
> Time and the hour run through the roughest day.

No sooner do we recognize and adapt to a given set of circumstances, than they become a thing of the past, a moment in time.

Instantly we are confronted with a completely new situation.

"The whole life of man is but a point of time," said Plutarch. And the life of man is no greater or more significant than any given moment in the succession of days we consider our allotted total.

"Live this day as if it were your last" has often been quoted as good advice. Equally good is the admonition, "Live this day as if it were your finest opportunity to achieve what your heart and mind really desire."

How to Have a Happy Family

When astronaut Frank Borman returned from his historic flight to the moon, newsmen wanted to know what reaction his young son had displayed. The astronaut smilingly replied that his boy was "magnificently unimpressed."

That sounds like a wholesome father-son relationship, the kind that most households would prefer to have—and it raises the question, what makes a happy family?

Youngsters and their parents are generally most contented in a home that runs like a benevolent monarchy. It is foolish to expect a family to operate as a pure democracy when children are small and must be carefully guided and disciplined. Instead, mothers and fathers should strive to have a household in which opinions are welcome and discussion is free—*but* it should be understood that the parental decision is final and must be obeyed. As children grow older, the parental power can and should relax, and the home move continually toward becoming a democracy.

It is imperative though that a home, to be happy, be a place of love, honesty and truth. Most kids can adjust to having a famous, or even an infamous, parent. It's their elders who sometimes cause trouble by disguising the truth in a misguided effort to protect their children and provide what they consider to be a more "normal" atmosphere.

Similarly, if a family member is sick or handicapped, children can accept this as a fact of life, providing their parents are intelligent enough to treat the matter rationally, and not as something to be denied or whispered about.

173

I am mindful of the notable careers of a man and woman who emerged from an impoverished background, he to climb to the presidency of a large corporation, and his sister to become a highly-respected educator.

Their father was a weak, nervous man, never able to make a decent living. The uneducated mother had to work at menial jobs to bring in money, so the time she could spend with her children was limited; yet, the son and daughter grew up as well-adjusted and eminently successful citizens. Why? When I asked the son this question, he said, "I think we licked our family problems by facing up to them. We never hid anything from one another. We never kidded ourselves about Dad's condition or the need for Mama to work. Everybody has to live under circumstances that are a combination of favorable and unfavorable. In our case, we were favored with a father who was a lovable if ineffectual man, and a mother who was a strong influence for good behavior, even when we weren't in her presence.

"You see," he concluded, "we came to understand and appreciate one another for what we were and not for what we might have been."

That family situation is unusual only in the high level of achievement registered by the children. Millions of households accomplish similar results every year, sending out into the world sons and daughters who have learned to accept handicaps as a natural part of living, and faults as the one universal gift bestowed on all human beings.

Together, parents and children can develop a profound and beautiful relationship, full of warmth and security. The family can be more than an autocracy of kinship. It can be a lively fraternity, a place of shared inspiration, laughter and radiant faith.

The family ought to be a learning-and-loving group that encourages active participation by all members. To be most successful, it should also be a training school, where the ideals and habits of a lifetime are planted and cultivated. Finally, I think of the family as a small, private club for going places and doing things together, with parents leading the way at work, play and prayer, setting examples for their children to follow.

The mother or father, who fears that too much sharing of thoughts and experiences with children will result in a loss of parental control, does not understand the true basis of wholesome family life. Any father should look forward to the day when he relinquishes control over his children completely. It should be a natural and logical emancipation that accompanies adulthood. Maturity comes most naturally to the youngster who has known both the limits of his freedoms and his restrictions. Teaching this kind of self-discipline and sound judgment requires that elders be neither too lenient nor too stern. It is a tough parental test to walk the line of reason, being careful not to demand blind obedience or to tolerate unreasoning defiance.

These extremes can best be avoided where child and parent not only love each other, but also develop a healthy regard for one another's opinions and feelings. It is this type of permissive atmosphere that can cause youngsters to become teachers as well as students, setting as well as following examples, contributing to the enrichment of the family while continuing to accept nourishment from it.

Parents know only too well the faults of their children. They may not be aware that their children know equally well the faults of the parents. If the shortcomings of both are candidly admitted, a good start can be made in establishing a sincere and satisfying family dialogue.

This by no means suggests that the daughter and son assume equal authority with the father and mother. It does recommend that parents be more willing to practice what they preach, to admit when they are wrong, and to demonstrate the same courtesy that they expect from their offspring. If children are expected to honor their father and mother, then parents should vow to honor their sons and daughters.

In many families there is too much parental posturing, too much sham and pretense. No wonder so many youngsters grow up calling their fathers phonies, and their mothers hypocrites! Parents need not be viewed as omnipotent ogres or indentured servants. They can be firm without antagonizing, generous without coddling, and fair without punishing.

Children, on the other hand, are not angels requiring over-protection, nor are they devils to be shunned. They are personalities worthy of attention, deserving of respect and capable of carrying out reasonable obligations and duties.

175

Unfortunately, in many homes across the nation, Mom, Dad and the kids are virtually strangers to one another. Communication is difficult to initiate and, when attempted, generally proves to be a painful disappointment. There is unwillingness to talk and impatience to listen.

Life is particularly galling to the adolescent, who is buffeted between his desire for independence and his feelings of dependence.

Every family member reflects in certain ways his own anxiety about the confusion that besets the world, and the home often becomes a natural repository for aggressions and pent-up emotions.

"My folks don't understand me and I certainly don't understand them," lamented a tenth-grade student who was participating in a panel discussion of teen-age problems. "They seem to have forgotten what it's like to be young."

I doubt that many mothers and fathers have forgotten their youth, but they think it's part of another life. They don't realize that as adults they should be merely older, and hopefully wiser, extensions of their former selves. From the vantage point of his years, the parent can look back to the time when he also was a youngster; and his reactions should favorably reflect that knowledge.

Of course, there's another complication in family relationships: that's the factor of kinship itself with all its delicate and sensitive nuances.

Let's face it. A child is incapable of judging his parents as he does other adults. He is too bound by ties of devotion and filial obligation to be objective. Parents, in turn, cannot look at their own sons and daughters with the same objectivity they reserve for other youngsters of the neighborhood.

But family members can still strive to effect a balance between love and justice, devotion and discipline, democracy and duty.

Many of the troubled people in this world are products of families in which relationships have deteriorated, and the needs of the individual have been warped or denied.

There are parents who can only possess. They seek in one way or another to enslave. Their children react either by submitting to parental dictatorship or, with increasing frequency, by revolting and renouncing all family ties and domination.

There is a better answer, well worth every family's efforts to achieve. It envisions parents and children placing intelligent limits on what they expect of one another, even though they may be unlimited in their love.

We are moving into an age of rapid change and new concepts about living that may show us how to meet some of our age-old obligations in fresh new ways. The physical form of the home itself will doubtlessly be different, with vast changes in heating, lighting, carpeting and furnishings, and major kitchen and sanitation improvements. With higher development of human sensitivity and awareness, the entire atmosphere of the home may change as well. This change may deepen the parent-child relationship, strengthening the faith of everyone in the household, and assuring a future of better-adjusted individuals and happier, more stable families.

The Simple Life

Are you old enough to remember the simple life? Growing up in a small town, I knew what it was like to go hunting in the woods for hickory nuts, to carve a slingshot from a piece of wood and tie to it rubber strips cut from an old inner tube. Instead of candy bars, we chewed sour apples and sugarcane and raw sweet potatoes. We played games such as marbles, mumblety-peg and checkers. Fun was rolling a worn-out tire, flying a kite made of dried stalks and newspaper, or soaring reasonably high in the air in a homemade backyard swing.

We didn't know much about buying games or toys in a store. You could always make up a game to play even if you were alone. When two or more playmates gathered, you had the makings of every kind of game from one-eyed cat to football.

Not everything was joy and happiness in those days. We grew up knowing more than we cared to about poverty, unemployment and hungry families; houses with broken windows, leaking roofs and peeling paint. There was a certain sad, gray loneliness about life in the depression days. Machines didn't threaten man as they do today, for then they were often still and silent. Many factories were closed and dollars were hard to come by.

So the simple life was Spartan as well, and we made do because we had to, but the experiences had some value for us. They taught us ingenuity and adaptability.

There is a singular lack of both qualities in many of today's generation. Why devise a game when you can buy one? Why make anything that is already manufactured and conveniently available? Why concern yourself with creating a purposeful existence when money can purchase almost anything you need or want?

These are typical questions that a bored and affluent youngster might very well ask. Instead of dreaming up and creating some diversion, he has so many places to go, so much to see and do, he often has trouble only in making up his mind.

But like the corpulent child who eats too much chocolate candy, a person can get sick from having more of everything than he knows how to use profitably: more time, more money, more recreation than he can enjoy, more advantages than he could possibly use. When the appetite becomes jaded and the future holds no challenge, a despondent person might well conclude that the age of plenty is the age of barren loneliness.

Doesn't this account for many of the cases of misdirected young lives that come to our attention constantly: the seekers for a new and deeper awareness who wander off in many directions exploring erotic and bizarre avenues of self-identification and expression? And what of the thousands who find no answers despite their most persistent and frantic efforts, and so conclude their search by committing suicide?

One of the greatest lessons in life is learning to be happy without things we shouldn't have, or cannot have. The difficulty arises in teaching this to persons who refuse to learn except by bitter experience. It may be that this is the only effective way to learn it.

In earlier days of economic hardship and social primitivism, individuals found out that fulfillment in life could only come from realizing that one makes his own happiness. True, you can buy material possessions, but you can't buy satisfaction, serenity or inner strength.

One should not seek escape from troubles, but confrontations with them. Human beings are born to meet difficulties and make decisions. There is as much need today for the pioneering spirit as there was a century ago, only the frontier is not now a geographical one; but it is no less challenging, and even more promising in the rewards it offers. Mankind must pioneer in human relations, in matching himself with his machines, and in finding the spiritual qualities that are too often hidden in a materialistic civilization.

The future is not hopeless, and we inhabitants of this atomic age are not helpless. Everyone on this earth has within his genes a burning desire for love, acceptance, and accomplishment, just as did the simple people of a simpler age.

We must trust ourselves to find new meaning in our existence by learning again to be constructively and personally innovative. Regardless of how complicated life becomes, it still must be reduced to basic essentials if it is to have any meaning and provide any lasting satisfaction for the individual.

Learn to Laugh

How's your sense of humor? If you're on the receiving end of a joke, does it flatter you or make you nervous? When the fellow next door says, "Hi, Blimp," do you appreciate the suggestion that you need to lose some weight; or do you resent the jibe as an unwarranted invasion of your privacy?

The way you react to jokes tells what the language of humor conveys to you, and it also reveals much about your attitude and your self-confidence. If you like to laugh, then humor is probably a basic commodity in your life; and you doubtlessly rely on jokes as a happy supplement to conversation. On the other hand, you may be wary of trading jokes because you recognize the ability of the humorous thrust to cut through to the heart of a matter. "Many a true word is spoken in jest," is a sound observation. Jokes, satire, sarcasm are all methods of telling the truth in a special manner. The court jester traditionally was the one person able to be perfectly frank with the king and still protect his head because of the cleverness of his tongue. If humor is well-handled, it need not be painful. It can be an effective method of communication and a source of real enjoyment. The best quipsters have the ability to sugarcoat their words so that the result is gentle and almost affectionate.

Learning to accept a joke graciously and to tell one masterfully are both accomplishments well worth your time and attention! Public relations counselors advise clients to tell it with humor whenever they can. Putting on a glum face and talking in terms of grim statistics is likely to put people to sleep or in a fighting mood. If you want to make some positive points, try the way of laughter.

This is not a new idea. The Bible tells us in the Psalms that God knows how to laugh and has put gladness into mankind. Students of the Scriptures can point to many humorous passages, some emphasizing irony and others good-natured fun.

The ancient poet Horace recommended that we live in love and laughter, and a succession of later scribes brought the art of comic writing to a high degree of professionalism. Some of the caricatures and satirical jibes in Shakespeare's plays have never been surpassed.

It is important to note, however, that humor which impresses itself upon the mind and has lasting value concerns real persons and their shortcomings. A joke is really no joke, even though it is a laughing matter. It is a humorous viewpoint on a very real person and his problems.

Abraham Lincoln understood humor and how to use it in masterful fashion. So did Adlai Stevenson. Both of these great Americans were best at teasing themselves, for they did not fear humor but used it as an artist uses colors—to make life brighter and more interesting.

Mark Twain was in many ways the greatest humorist America has ever produced. He could be delicate or caustic, puckish or satanic. His lectures were laugh-filled exposures of virtually every fault man possesses.

Some years ago Will Rogers developed his humorous talents to a high degree, and millions would tune in weekly to hear his laugh-provoking comments on the newsmakers of the day. Contemporary humorists who have won great fame knocking the stuffing out of stuffed shirts include Bob Hope, Flip Wilson, Don Rickles, and Al Capp.

Each in his own way is able to poke fun with a deft touch. Often they deal with the most serious matters and criticize individuals in high places, but they do it with such finesse that the public finds their performance highly entertaining. Even the victims of their verbal assaults are often flattered to be given so much publicity.

It is well to remember, however, that many people are sensitive about teasing. They may enjoy hearing funny comments about others but not about themselves. So giving someone repeated little digs can be one of the surest ways to bury a friendship.

This doesn't mean that you should stop telling jokes, only that you handle humor with the proper respect for its power. Anyone who resents teasing will hardly see anything harmless or kindly about being the butt of a joke or a satirical comment.

A. N. Whitehead even went so far as to label satire, "The soured milk of human kindness." Art Buchwald tells of receiving letters every day from readers who think his off-beat writings are serious, malicious, and completely factual; so humor is not only resented by some but thoroughly misunderstood by many others.

Yet, the wisecrack and the gibe and the funny story do have a place in our lives. If we listen carefully and not too nervously, we can even derive understanding and knowledge. "People learn while they laugh," wrote Frank Moore Colby, "but very few of them know that they are learning."

"My way of joking is telling the truth," said dramatist George Bernard Shaw. "That is the funniest joke in the world." Certainly the jest and the funny story have been used effectively for centuries to deflate the pompous and prod the indifferent. Laughter has been lauded as an aid to digestion, a way to make friends, a dispeller of gloom and a requisite for remaining young and optimistic. Abraham Lincoln considered laughter to be "the joyous, universal evergreen of life." Year in and year out, humor continues to be one of the most popular ingredients of television programs, books and plays.

Jokes and laughter even express the spirit of a nation. People with a grim outlook rarely use humor. There is said to be relatively little laughter in totalitarian states because life is a serious business. Hardly anyone dares to poke fun at the government or the people in it. A flip remark, regardless of how slight its content, could lead to one's undoing. By contrast, free people tend to laugh freely, refusing to take themselves too seriously or to be unduly nervous about their destiny. This is good and desirable.

The famous actress Ethel Barrymore noted that "You grow up the day you have your first real laugh at yourself," and comedian Bill Cosby has made a fortune recalling the universal humor exhibited by members of his own family.

Our best chance for finding happiness is by looking for it on the funny side of life. We do not stop laughing because we grow old; we grow old because we stop laughing.

Faith and the Future

How Religious Are You?

Who is the most religious person you know? Does any name come
to mind? If it does, you might consider why you suddenly thought
of a particular individual and the yardstick you employed in making
your choice. It might give you a clue to your own faith and how
religious you are.

Many of us have a rather elementary conception of what it means
to be religious. Our judgment may be based on childhood memories
and Sunday School lessons that emphasized attending worship services, reading the Bible and, on occasion, publicly professing one's
faith. All of these acts of consecration may be, and doubtlessly often
are, legitimate evidence of an inspired and dedicated spirit. On the
other hand, they could mean nothing. I am sure that you know more
than one person who makes a great pretense of being devout, but
who does pitifully little to prove it. On the other hand, many charitable and compassionate persons go unnoticed because they are

deliberately quiet and unobtrusive about the good deeds they perform.

This points up one of the difficulties in trying to decide whether someone is religious or not. The most personal matter in the world is each individual's inner being. It is impossible to know the full depth and breadth of anyone's beliefs about God. When one person accuses another of being irreligious, he only marks himself as being both ill-mannered and irresponsible, for he is attempting to judge a relationship he knows nothing about. We are never justified in going any farther than Arnold Toynbee's speculation that religion is an intrinsic faculty of human nature. "I believe that being human involves having religion and any human beings who declare that they have no religion are deceiving themselves through failing to search their own hearts."

Even this may be an unjustified criticism to level at another individual (for we can never be sure that someone who claims to be a nonbeliever really is) or even that he means what he says.

History abounds with true stories about persons who have had their lives transformed by some overwhelming spiritual experience. Suddenly an irreligious skeptic finds himself profoundly believing in God. Are we to assume that such an individual had no faith until miraculously it flew into his consciousness like a mystical bird, or would it not be more plausible to suggest that the ingredients of faith were inside him all the time and needed only to be brought together like the rapid combining of minute particles in an atomic reactor?

If we truly want to know those among us who are deeply religious, we might try looking for the inspired and the inspiring among us who are living by the Golden Rule. We also should keep a lookout for those who deliver beautiful, unspoken prayers with their kind acts of charity; helping the sick and the poor, the ignorant and the downtrodden.

How religious is anyone? As religious as he alone feels, and decides in his own mind and heart and soul. It is a secret that each of us must and can share only with God.

Prayers That Work

High above the ocean the passengers of the jet plane were told by their pilot that one of the engines had failed. "Well, we'd better start to pray," said an alarmed young man. His seatmate raised his eyebrows and asked, "Do you think it's that bad?" That reaction to an apocryphal situation is sadly representative of many persons who consider religion as a handy tool, and prayer as emergency equipment to be used in time of need.

Religion must be deeper and more substantial than that to satisfy most of today's conscientious men and women. They have seen too many instances of the kind person struck down by sudden disaster, and the evil opportunist benefiting from his illegal and immoral efforts, to believe that simple prayer will make right what is wrong or insure safety to the imperiled.

We don't live in that kind of world, and many youngsters, especially, are rebelling against a shallow theology that declares you need only have faith and think positively in order to get what you want from life.

To have faith is not to possess or be possessed by any automatic problem-solver. In fact, if religion teaches us anything it should be that there are no easy answers in this world, no escapes from inevitable sorrows, no way of avoiding your share of responsibilities, troubles and tragedies. Faith of the right kind can help us to accept our human limitations as not only bearable, but as a challenge to outstanding humanitarian achievements.

> Is not religion all deeds and all reflection . . . ?
> . . . Who can separate his faith from his actions, or his beliefs from his occupations?
> Who can spread his hours before him, saying, "This for God and this for myself; This for my soul, and this other for my body"? . . .
> . . . Your daily life is your temple and your religion.
>
> Kahlil Gibran in *The Prophet*

Today, as never before, religion is coming to be recognized as a daily personal matter, rather than an occasional impersonal one. The dedicated man of faith is looking to his own religion to help him change the world, to bring peace to mankind, to draw black and white men together as brothers, to remove from the atmosphere the crackling sparks of greed, envy and hate that so often flame into violence. The man of faith also realizes that peace must start within his own being, that brotherly love be generated within his own mind and conscience. In short, prayers that work are religion in action.

Anyone who becomes conscious of the responsibility he bears toward another human being has learned the why of his existence and the essence of his religion. He has been lifted from the ranks of the takers, who ask for special consideration in their prayers, to the higher echelon of the givers, who worship and ask only to be of help to others. His every act of goodness becomes an act of faith, for it expects and seeks no rewards.

Could it be that millions of conscientious and dedicated people, who may not be strong on church-going and hymn-singing, but who work actively for peace and show their love and concern for their fellow human beings in many unselfish ways, are leading the world to a new, exalted religious awakening?

Let us not dismiss the possibility. God is not dead. But He may be sitting back, happily watching as more and more of His children start at last to do some of the noble work they were put here for in the first place.

End of the World

If the people of the world were suddenly to learn that they had only one day to live, what would happen? I heard a speaker speculate about that possibility and suggest that the telephone lines would be jammed with millions of callers rushing to tell one another of their love, and of profound regret for past misdeeds and obligations left unmet.

It's a touching supposition and a heartwarming picture of mankind's true goodness made evident by crisis—but I doubt that it would be that way at all! If word came flashing by way of radio and television that the world was coming to an end, most people would simply use their telephones to check on the validity of the report. Then if convinced that the prediction were true, I suspect that most of the frightened and bewildered, and they would number into countless millions, would start running around crazily like so many ants on a hot skillet.

Never having felt any deep concern for their fellow man, the self-centered would hold true to form and worry only about themselves. Like a wild, howling typhoon they would roar into the streets and rampage across the countryside, many of them drunk and drugged and already half-scared to death. They would tear and rip and trample the earth so that by day's end the destruction would be virtually complete. The prophesy would be nearly complete except for man's eliminating himself by a combination of means, including murder, suicide and starvation.

But it's all make-believe, you say, so why give it a second thought? Is it a far-fetched story, a wild-eyed fantasy?

Listen to Arnold Toynbee: "Today Man finds himself genuinely in danger of being destroyed by a Frankenstein's monster which is the work of his own hands." If this is true and the explosive power in the hands of major nations is so enormous that all humanity could be blown away in minutes, then the signal has already been given. The world has been put on notice. The only information not divulged is the day of destruction.

And what are the people doing? Just about what we described. Perhaps the mobs in the streets are not quite as frantic or insane; but they are doing a rather complete job of ripping, tearing and trampling the good earth, and the reports of murders, suicides and mass starvation mount daily.

Thankfully, not everyone is so engrossed in finishing off himself and his world. There are some kind, gentle, rational souls left on this battered, old planet. They are the devoted mothers and fathers, the idealistic youngsters, the wise counselors of the pulpit who believe that there is still hope for man and time left to preserve his neck and his purpose in being here. Their reasoning probably sounds old-fashioned to the youthful cynics and impractical to the doddering skeptics, for it is based on such time-honored ideas as justice, mercy and brotherly love.

To the lonely and tormented, wandering around in confusion, groping fearfully in the darkness, the man of reason and faith says, "Find yourself, and then you will find your destiny."

It is true that every person must pay a price ultimately for his initial admittance to this world; but membership in the human family does not entitle anyone to live in idle numbness or superficial smugness, nor does it condemn anyone to a premature moral and spiritual death.

Every person has infinite capabilities. With his vast scientific knowledge, man can persevere and not perish, build instead of destroy. Professor Barrows Dunham has reasoned that men and women who have made other Utopian schemes come true can also achieve worldwide cooperation and peace. "The dreams men dream while waking can become the substance of a world."

Watching the rise and fall of many civilizations has made historian Toynbee uncertain about our future, but he sounds this hopeful challenge: "Our destiny is *not* predetermined for us; we determine it for ourselves. If we crash, it will be because we have chosen death and evil when we were free to choose life and good."

Ideas for Tomorrow

"The philosophies of our age have become the absurdities of the next, and the foolishness of yesterday has become the wisdom of tomorrow." A wise man named Sir William Osler said that, and many examples can be found to prove the paradox.

Notice how our thoughts about good and evil, race and religion, crime and punishment, are all undergoing profound changes. You need only study life of the nineteenth century to see the tremendous differences between the thinking of people then and their descendants of today. Grandfather was taught the virtues of hard work, thrift, minding his own business, and succeeding by individual effort. He put great emphasis on demonstrated morality, believing that one should attend church regularly, live quietly and circumspectly, teach his children to be seen and not heard, and refrain from any public show of affection, even for the members of his own family.

Contrast that with the modern American family. Permissive parents and emancipated children live in a totally different world. They tend to be outspoken, candid, quick to express opinions and show emotions. Many youngsters think hard work is not only unnecessary but a ridiculous waste of time and energy. Thrift is scoffed at because it merely ties up money that could be spent for pleasurable purposes. Yet for many the emphasis now *is* less on striving for one's own selfish attainments and more on working with others to make life better for everyone.

This is a brash generation and its members do not hesitate to ridicule anything they consider evil, foolish, archaic or unnecessary. Were the mothers and fathers of the past all wrong, and are today's uninhibited millions correct in everything they believe and in how they behave? The answer to both questions, of course, is no. There's something to be said for and against both the "folly" of the past and the "errors" of the present.

Each generation rebels against the established order and calls for a new set of rules, confident that it has found better answers to the questions besetting the world.

Centuries ago each Egyptian pharaoh must have believed that civilization had reached its highest mark under his reign. Several of the rulers of ancient Greece and Rome felt that they had solved most of the problems of their day and had charted mankind on a bold, new course to take care of all his future needs.

Genghis Khan, Alexander the Great and Julius Caesar, each in his heyday thought that he embodied the ultimate answer to the world's

189

need for leadership. Adolph Hitler was so imbued with the power and permanence of his mad philosophy that he made plans to perpetuate his social order at least for a thousand years, even dictating the design of special buildings to house the government as he envisioned it should be long after he was dead! In the intervening years since Hitler's downfall, German youth have realized that his theories were not just absurd, but bestial and horribly savage. Children of goose-stepping storm troopers know that what their parents accepted as Nazi "wisdom" was actually the mouthings of a madman.

Edward R. Murrow, the radio and TV commentator, was fond of saying, "The greatest friend of truth is time." Perhaps we can never see all the absurdities of our own generation, because we are participants in the environment; and our foolishness can only be recognized by more objective observers at a later date.

Each individual is imprisoned within the years of his own awareness and involvement, and much of what we accept as correct appears so only because we cannot imagine any other state of affairs being more logical. Despite the many changes that have occurred within recent years in our styles of dress and modes of living and behaving, it is still difficult for anyone to project himself far enough into the future to visualize a time when people will speak a different language, travel in fantastic machines at or near the speed of light, eat strange foods, live under the ocean or on distant planets, and respect perhaps different social and ethical values.

What, then, is the lasting value? Does anything have permanence, or will all basic beliefs in time come to be inanities and drivel? There is overwhelming evidence that the principles we hold dearest are adaptable to any age and any civilization. The Ten Commandments and the Golden Rule are undiminished by the passing of time. They never grow old, never lose their lustre and meaning. Each new generation searches for ways to define morality and ethical values. The words may differ and the methods used to describe the still, small voice of conscience may vary; but there is a universal and everlasting validity to goodness, righteousness and generosity.

In the dawning days of man's arrival on this planet, he became aware of the desirability of peace and the blessings of brotherly love. He has not ceased to yearn for both, although he has shown little disposition to make either one a reality. Nevertheless, man's highest aspirations have not changed. His hope is to be better than he is, and his dream is to make of his world a better place. The simple and basic guide lines for achieving these goals are at our fingertips. They will still be available a century or a millennium from now—and as long as mankind exists.